THEMATIC UNIT
Plants

Written by
Mary Ellen Sterling

Teacher Created Resources, Inc.
6421 Industry Way
Westminster, CA 92683
www.teachercreated.com

ISBN: 978-1-55734-244-7

©1995 Teacher Created Resources, Inc.
Reprinted, 2008

Made in U.S.A.

Teacher Created Resources

Edited by
Pamela Friedman

Illustrated by
Agi Palinay

Cover Art by
Blanca Apodaca LaBounty

Table of Contents

Introduction

Plants contains four captivating whole language thematic units. Its 80 exciting pages are filled with a wide variety of lesson ideas and reproducible pages designed for use at the early childhood level. At its core are four high quality children's literature selections. For each of these books, activities are included which set the stage for reading, encourage the enjoyment of the book, and extend the concepts gained.

The theme of *Plants* is connected to the curriculum with activities in language arts, math, science, social studies, art, music, movement, and life skills. Many of these activities encourage cooperative learning. Suggestions and patterns for bulletin boards are additional time savers for the busy teacher. Furthermore, directions for student-created Big Books and culminating activities, which allow students to synthesize their knowledge in order to produce products that can be shared beyond the classroom, highlight this very complete teacher resource.

Included in this Thematic Unit

Literature Selections – summaries of four children's books with related lessons (complete with reproducible pages) that cross the curriculum.

Language Experiences and Writing Ideas – various activities that cross the curriculum, including Big Books.

Bulletin Board Ideas – plans for student-created and/or interactive bulletin boards.

Homework Suggestions – ways to extend the unit to the child's home.

Curriculum Connections – activities in language arts, math, science, social studies, art, music, movement, and life skills.

Group Projects – ideas to foster cooperative awareness and prepare for cooperative learning.

Culminating Activities – projects which require students to synthesize their learning to produce a product or engage in an activity that can be shared with others.

Bibliography – listings of additional related fiction and nonfiction books.

Suggested Activity Centers

Storytime – a place to sit comfortably while reading and discussing books.

Reading – where children can read books and poems related to the unit on their own and practice reading-related activities.

Art – where children can draw, color, paint, cut, and paste to express their thoughts and feelings.

Science – a place for experimenting and discovering.

Plant – a place for planting and growing.

Math – a place for learning counting, sequencing, math, and problem solving.

Dramatic Play – where children use imagination and props to act out ideas.

Outdoors – used to promote large muscle development and to extend learning outside the classroom.

Introduction *(cont.)*

Why Whole Language?

In a whole language program, activities are arranged around a literacy experience. Children become involved in all modes of communication: reading, writing, listening, observing, illustrating, and experiencing. Communication skills are interconnected and integrated into lessons that emphasize the whole of language rather than its isolated parts. Reading is not taught as a separate subject from writing and spelling, for example. A child reads, writes (spelling appropriately for his/her level), speaks, listens, etc. in response to a story or poems introduced by the teacher. In this way, language skills grow naturally, stimulated by involvement and interest in the topic at hand.

Why Thematic Planning?

Thematic planning is a useful tool for implementing a whole language program. By choosing a theme with correlating literature selections for a unit of study, a teacher can plan activities throughout the day that lead to a cohesive, in-depth study of the topic. Students practice and apply their skills in meaningful contexts. Consequently, they tend to learn and retain more. Both teachers and students are freed from a day that is broken into unrelated segments of isolated drill and practice.

Why Prepare for Cooperative Learning?

In addition to academic skills, students need to learn social skills to function well in modern society. The foundation for successful social skills can be built in early childhood. By introducing whole-class activities, a teacher can create a cooperative awareness and attitude in the classroom. Whole-class activities are especially important in creating a comfortable, safe environment in which students have some knowledge and understanding of each other. Once this is established, children can go on to work in pairs and then in groups. They will be ready to succeed in future cooperative learning situations.

Why Big Books?

The production of Big Books is an excellent cooperative, whole language activity. The entire class can apply their language skills, content knowledge, and creativity to produce a Big Book that can become a part of the classroom library to be read and reread. These books made splendid culminating projects for sharing beyond the classroom with family, friends, librarians, other classes, etc.

How a Seed Grows

by Helene J. Jordan

Summary

This book was originally published in 1960, yet it is as timely as ever. Engaging updated illustrations that feature multicultural characters add to its relevance and usability for a wider audience.

As the title states, the topic of this book is seeds and how they grow. First, different types of seeds are pictured and examined. Then the reader is guided through a step-by-step bean-planting experiment in which he may actively participate. Accompanying the text are illustrations of the developing seed. The third concept presented in the book takes a look at what plants need in order to grow.

The simplified language along with the softly colored illustrations will surely appeal to young learners and provide a fitting introduction to a unit on seeds.

Overview of Activities

Setting the Stage

Bulletin Board. Assemble and display the Rainbow of Flowers Bulletin Board. (See pages 75 to 79 for directions and patterns.)

Plant Center. Bring in a number of live plants and display all of them at a special plant center. If you do not have any spare tables, set up an ironing board or use a large window sill and arrange the plants on it. You may want to include herbs (which can be easily grown or purchased at a grocery store), flowers, and even plants started from carrot or potato cuttings.

Reading. Provide a wide variety of subject-related reading materials for the children. The Bibliography on page 80 contains a number of outstanding books from which to choose. Also, look in past copies of *Ranger Rick or Chickadee* for articles about plants and growing things. If you desire, place all the books, pamphlets, etc., in a basket underneath the table, ironing board, or window sill. Then add some throw pillows nearby to create a cozy book nook.

Background Information. Establish some background information about plants by using What Is a Plant? on page 8. Follow up and/or assess the children's learning with the other activities on that same page.

Edible Prompt. Give each child a small amount of unsalted sunflower seeds. Direct them to set one seed aside to observe while you talk about it. Allow them to eat the other sunflower seeds while you read aloud *How a Seed Crows.*

Overview of Activities *(cont.)*

Enjoying the Story

Read Aloud. Read aloud *How a Seed Grows.* Allow plenty of time for students to look at the pictures as you read.

Story Review. Review the story with some discussion questions and writing activities. For your reference, sample questions and answers are provided on page 9.

Seed Knowledge. Direct the children's attention to the lone sunflower seed that each saved earlier. (If any were accidentally eaten, provide replacements.) Then ask them to tell what they know about seeds. Record their responses on chart paper. Have the children draw pictures of the plants their seeds would become if they were to be planted and successfully grown.

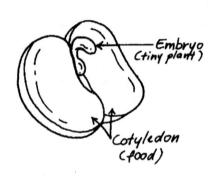

Grown Plants. Draw and label pictures of some other kinds of seeds that were mentioned in the story (acorn, beans). Have the children tell what kinds of plants the seeds will grow into (or let them draw pictures).

Phonics. With the class, brainstorm a list of words that have the same long e sound as seed (or that rhyme with the word seed). Record all responses on chart paper. Tell the children to write and illustrate two words that have the same long e sound (or that rhyme with the word seed).

Opposites. Some seeds grow slowly while others grow fast. Explore the meanings of the opposites fast and slow. Choose two children, one to be fast and the other to be slow. At a given signal, tell them to walk from the back of the room to the front, using the proper speed. Enact some other opposites.

Science and Math. Plant some seeds. Follow the directions outlined in the story or use a different seed-growing method. (Four alternatives are described on page 10.)

Have children participate in the following three activities.

* Examine the seeds daily and draw pictures of the progress made each day.
* Count the number of seeds that are growing, then draw the same number of seedlings.
* Write science reports about the planting experience. (Some sample report forms can be found on page 11.)

Math Fun. Ten different math activities are described on pages 12 and 13. Immediately following are two pages of flannel board rhymes (page 14) and patterns (page 15) for counting, adding, and subtracting. Use those ideas which best suit your classroom needs.

Overview of Activities *(cont.)*

Extending the Story

Drama and Movement. Combine creative drama and movement with this activity. Tell the students the story of how a seed grows. As you do so, have them reenact the seed as it goes through the various stages of growth. Play soft music in the background to enhance the mood. A sample script follows.

* I am the seed. (Children curl up into a ball on the floor.)
* When I am planted in soil a root begins to grow. (Have the children straighten out one leg.)
* My job as a root is to reach underground and suck up water and vitamins from the soil. (Children can make slurping noises.)
* Pretty soon hair roots begin to grow from my root. (Have the children slowly uncurl their other leg.)
* A bud begins to push up through the ground. (Children lift up their heads and push upwards.)
* Soon, leaves form. (Children spread out their arms.)

Seed Life Cycle. Make a seed life cycle chart. Using a black marker, divide a paper plate into fourths. Instruct the children to write a numeral from one to four in each space (see diagram at right). As a class, review the four stages of growth for a seed. List them (in short sentence format) on the board for all to see. Have the children copy the correct sentence in each space and draw an illustration for each one.

No Seeds. Some plants do not grow from seeds. You may want to explore the fascinating pictures and facts in the book *Plants That Never Ever Bloom* by Ruth Heller (Grosset & Dunlap, 1984). Assign each group of children a different mural. One group can draw an ocean scene of seaweed; another can draw a circle of different kinds of mushrooms, etc. They may also play a game with the cards on page 16 (directions on page).

Listening. Listen to "The Seed Cycle" on cassette from the album *Wee Sing and Play* published by Price Stern Sloan. Have everyone learn the words and music.

Art. Art projects can include an S for seed mosaic, a seed bracelet, a seeded box, or a seed pin. All the materials and directions are outlined on page 17.

Literature Selections. See page 20 for three fine literature selections that can be used to introduce, extend, or culminate a unit of study on seeds.

Little Books. Children can make little books about plants to take home and share with their families. See page 18 for a sample book; directions can be found on page 19.

What Is a Plant?

To help the children distinguish between plants and nonplants you may want to implement the following lesson. Gather a number of live plants and some examples of nonplants to show the class. Then follow the steps in the procedure below. Appropriate homework and follow-up activity ideas are also supplied.

Materials: Any number of live plants such as a flowering plant, an herb, and a plant from a cutting; nonplant items such as a hairbrush, a crayon, and a live insect in a glass jar

Directions:

* Display all the plants and nonplants on a table or cart. Have the children identify each item.
* Tell the children to group together all the things that can grow.
* Ask them to tell what makes things that grow alike. (They need food; they need water; they are alive, etc.)
* Call attention to the insect. How is it different from the other things that grow? (It can move from place to place by itself; it can go in search of its own food, etc.)
* Remove the insect from the group and establish that the remaining things are called plants.
* Place all the plants in the classroom plant center.

Follow-Up Activities

* Make a chart which identifies some of the characteristics of a plant. Display it at the Plant Center.
* Discuss some of the following topics: Ways We Use Plants; Different Ways Plants Grow; What Plants Need to Grow. Answers for these and other topics can be found in *Plants We Know* by O. Irene Sevrey Miner (Children's Press, 1981).
* For a homework assignment, have the children draw pictures of plants and nonplants around their homes or neighborhoods. Share the findings with the whole group; ask the children to explain why each is or is not a plant.
* Here are two alternative ideas for the above activity.

1. Have the children cut pictures of plants and nonplants from old magazines. Paste the pictures on a classroom chart labeled Plants and Nonplants.

2. Take the class on a short nature walk. Before heading outdoors, pair the children and instruct each pair to find and collect a plant and a nonplant. Upon returning to the classroom have them share their findings with the rest of the class.

Discussion and Writing Activities

Use any or all of the following discussion questions and writing activities to review and reinforce concepts in the story *How a Seed Grows*. Sample answers have been supplied for quick reference. Writing activities have been starred (*). The questions may be used during circle time.

1. What is a seed? *(a little plant that has not started to grow)*
   * Have the children copy a simple sentence: A seed is a little plant that has not started to grow.

2. Name some things that grow from seeds. *(apple trees, daisies, carrots, corn, clover, wheat, etc.)*
   * Tell the students to write the names of two plants that grow from seeds.

3. Name a seed that grows slowly. *(oak tree)*
   Name a seed that grows fast. *(bean seed)*

4. In the story what was used to plant seeds? *(eggshells)*
   What other things could be used to plant seeds? *(tin cans, old cups, or little flowerpots)*
   * Tell the children to draw a picture of something they would choose as a container for planting seeds.

5. How did they make holes in the eggshells? *(with a pencil)*

6. How many eggshells did they fill? *(12)*
   * Practice writing the number names from one to twelve.

7. After they made a hole in the soil what did they do? *(planted a bean seed in it and covered it with soil)*

8. What did they sprinkle on the soil? *(a little water)*
   * Have the children *(in pairs)* dictate and write directions telling how to plant a seed.

9. Each shell was numbered. How many were there? *(12)*

10. After putting the eggshells in an egg carton, where did they place the carton? *(on a window sill in sunlight)*

11. How often should the seeds be watered? *(a little every day)*

12. What does the water do? *(soaks into the seeds and the seeds begin to grow)*

13. When should seed number 1 be dug up? *(after three days)*

14. How long should you wait to dig up seed number 2? *(two more days)*

15. What part of the seed starts to grow first? *(root)*

16. What do you call the tiny roots growing from the big root? *(root hairs)*

17. What do the root hairs do? *(push down into the soil)*

18. What do the bean seeds do? *(push up through the soil)*

19. What do the shoots grow towards? *(the sun)*
    * Have the children draw and label the parts of a bean plant. *(the seed, root, root hairs, shoot, and the leaves)*

20. What three things does a plant need to grow? *(soil, water, sun)*
    *Write these two sentences on the board: Plants need three things to grow. They are _____ , _____ , and _____ . Tell the children to copy the words and fill in the blanks.

Seed-Growing Methods

If you do not want to follow the seed-growing method described in the story *How a Seed Grows* here are four more ideas for you to try. The children may be paired or grouped for these projects.

A Sponge Planter

Materials: Natural sponge, lawn seed or bird seed, aluminum pie pan, water

Directions:

* Place the sponge in the center of the pie pan.
* Wet the sponge a little and sprinkle it with the seeds.
* Pour a thin layer of water into the pan. Check the water level daily. The sponge needs to stay moist.
* Seeds should sprout within a few days.

Variation: Use regular sponges instead of the natural ones. With scissors cut the sponges into circles, squares, stars, moons, or other shapes. Wet the sponge and squeeze out excess water before sprinkling it with seeds. Keep the sponge moist.

A Pine Cone Planter

Materials: Pine cones, lawn seed and/or small flower seeds, lids from large plastic margarine cups, water, play clay

Directions:

* Flatten a small ball of clay against the bottom of the pine cone. Press it firmly onto the plastic lid.
* Sprinkle the seeds on as many sections of the pine cone as possible.
* Fill the lid with water; check the water level daily and watch for sprouting seeds.

Avocado Plant

Avocado seeds are easy to sprout, and the plants can grow to be quite tall!

Materials: Avocado seeds, a nail, toothpicks, glasses of water

Directions:

* Use the nail to make three holes around the middle of the avocado seed.
* Push a toothpick securely into each hole.
* Place the avocado so that the three toothpicks balance on the rim of the glass while the bottom of the avocado remains in the water.
* Keep the avocado seed in a bright sunny spot. Watch it grow!

Cactus

Cactus seeds may be slow growing so you may want to demonstrate how to graft two cacti.

Materials: Potted moon cactus, any other small species of cactus, knife, grafting tape, wax

Directions:

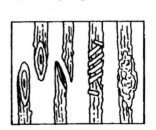

* Cut a diagonal section off of the potted cactus.
* Cut a section of the other cactus on the diagonal so it fits onto the section of the potted cactus.
* Wrap with grafting tape to hold together.
* Cover the grafted area with wax.

Plant Reports

After the children have planted seeds, you may want them to report on the growth progress as it occurs. On this page you will find a number of ideas for you to use.

Sample Form

Use the sample form below as a guideline for a plant report. Copy the text onto regular copy paper or make a class-size chart and fill it with everyone's observations.

My Plant Report

Directions: Write or draw about your plant experiment in each space.

These are the things I used:	This is what I did:

On _____ I
          (day)
checked my plant. This is how it looked:

On _____ I
          (day)
checked my plant. This is how it looked:

Accordion Books

Tape several sheets of construction paper together and fold accordion-style. On each page write a different day and date along with the children's observations. You may have pairs work together on this project. They can draw pictures, write sentences, or dictate their words for you to write.

Wheels

Cut out large circles from construction paper or tagboard. Divide them into fourths. Have each child record four observations from four different days in each of the segments (see diagram).

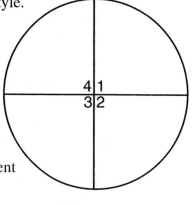

Math Fun

Math can easily be incorporated and correlated to a unit of studies on plants. Here are some suggestions for you to try.

1. **Sets of Twelve.** Each child will need one large index card, glue or paste, and some seeds (or dry beans). Tell the children to count out twelve seeds. After checking to make sure they each have twelve, tell them to glue the seeds to the index card. Have them write the number twelve on the front of the card. Note: This process can be repeated for any set you determine.

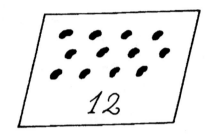

2. **Drawing Sets. Note:** The children may need some help with the first part of this activity, or you may want to prepare the sheets ahead of time. Fold a sheet of drawing paper in half (make a hot dog fold) and then in thirds.

   Open up the paper. Demonstrate to the children how to number each space from one to six on the front and from seven to twelve on the back. In each space have them draw the appropriate number of seeds (or other figures).

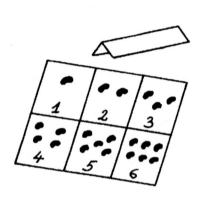

3. **Egg Cup Sets.** Collect a number of break apart plastic eggs. Write a different numeral from one to twelve (or any number you may choose) on the outside of each cup. Supply the child with a handful of dry beans, seeds, or cereal. Instruct the child to fill each cup with the number of beans that is written on the outside of the egg cup.

4. **Counting Sticks.** Make a set of seed counting sticks out of seeds (or dry beans), glue, and twelve wooden tongue depressors. Glue one seed to the first tongue depressor, two seeds to the second tongue depressor, and so on, until you have twelve counting sticks.

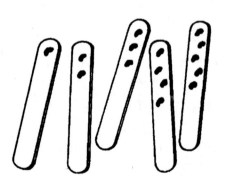

   * Let the children arrange them in correct numerical order.

   * Distribute the twelve counting sticks. Then call out a number; the child with that stick stands up.

   * Distribute the twelve counting sticks. Tell those students to arrange themselves in correct numerical order. Have them say their number names aloud.

5. **Counting.** With the students, count from one to twelve. Write the numbers from one to twelve on the board and point to each one as you count. Call on different children to count twelve hands, twelve chairs, etc. Count to twelve on a clock. Count the twelve egg cups in an egg carton. (You may want to include a brief introduction and definition of the word dozen at this time.)

Math Fun *(cont.)*

6. **Sorting**. Give each child a handful of a variety of seeds and beans. Direct children to sort the seeds and beans into like groups according to shape, color, and size.

7. **One-to-One Correspondence**.

Materials: A handful of beans (dry kidney, navy, white) or corn for each child, any color crayon, and paper plates

Directions:

   * Tell the children to draw twelve circles on the plate.
   * Have them place one bean in each circle.
   * Tell them to count the number of beans.

8. **Egg Carton Games.**

Materials: Egg carton, colored construction paper, rubber cement, marking pen, self-stick dots, seeds or beans

Directions:

   * Cover the top of the egg carton with colored construction paper cut to fit; attach the paper with rubber cement.
   * Write some simple directions on the cover, if desired.
   * On each colored self-sticking dot write a number from one to twelve; randomly attach them to the inside of the egg cup bottoms.
   * The children can fill each egg carton cup with the correct number of seeds (or beans).
   * For variety, have them match one of the counting sticks (see #4 on page 12) to its corresponding number.

9. **Pairs and Groups**. With the children, discuss things that come in pairs and groups. Draw or view a pair of pants, a pair of scissors, a pair of socks or mittens, etc. Have the children look through nature magazines for pictures of groups – a school of fish, a pride of lions, a flock of birds, etc. Review how many are in a dozen. Make a list of things that come in dozens – a dozen eggs, a dozen doughnuts, a dozen cookies, etc.

   * Count to twelve out loud with the children.
   * Have them practice writing the word name twelve and the numeral 12.
   * Finally, have children design their own creative sets of twelve.

10. **Flannel Board Patterns**. Construct the egg cup flannel board patterns on page 15. Use them for the counting exercises outlined on page 14.

Flannel Board Math

Construct the flannel board patterns on the following page (page 15). The egg cups can be used in any of the following math plays. Other suggested activities for the patterns are provided on page 15.

Counting in a Row

You will need 12 egg cups for this activity. Place the 12 patterns in a row on the flannel board. Say the following rhyme.

> Twelve little seeds all in a row
> Count how many plants we will grow.
> 1-2-3-4-5-6-7-8-9-10-11-12.

For subsequent verses line up as many egg cup patterns as you want the children to count.

Counting Backwards

Make as many egg cup patterns as you will need for this exercise. Line up the patterns in one row on the flannel board. Repeat the following rhyme. (Ten has been chosen for demonstration purposes only; you may choose any number you would like.)

> Ten little seeds all in a row.
> Count them down. Here we go.
> 10-9-8-7-6-5-4-3-2-1.

Addition

Here is an easy flannel board addition game. Make a set of seeds and then add another set. Say the following rhyme as you manipulate the seeds. (Five seeds have been added to two seeds for demonstration purposes only; you may use any numbers you choose.)

> Five little seeds, each in a cup.
> Here are two more. Add them all up
> 1-2-3-4-5-6-7.

Subtraction

This subtraction game is similar to the addition game above. One is taken away from each subsequent verse, but you may choose to begin with any number. The rhyme goes like this:

> Twelve little seeds
> All in a row. (Line up 12 seeds on the flannel board.)
> Take one away. (Remove one egg cup from the flannel board.)
> Count as you go.
> 1-2-3-4-5-6-7-8-9-10-11. (Have the children count the remaining seeds.)

Note: These games may be played individually. Supply each child with a handful of large beans. The children can make sets (on their own flannel boards) and count as they say the rhymes.

Patterns for Flannel Board Math

Directions: Make as many copies of this page as you will need. Color, cut out, and glue to tagboard. Laminate and trim. Attach a piece of sandpaper or felt to the back of each piece. Another option is to cut out patterns from felt or other fabrics. Then glue a fabric or real seed onto each egg cup.

Suggested Uses:

* Flannel board math games can be found on the previous page (page 14).

* Retell the planting sequence in *How a Seed Grows*.

* Make finger puppets. Form a construction paper strip into a circle and staple the ends together. Attach the seed cup pattern to the band (see diagram).

Playing Cards

Directions:

1. Copy, color, laminate, and cut out the cards. Pairs of students can practice identifying the plants and telling something about each one. (You may want to cover up the names before copying or cover temporarily during identification game.)

2. Make two copies of the cards below. Color, laminate, and cut out. Store in a labeled manila envelope when not in use. Children can play a game of concentration with the cards.

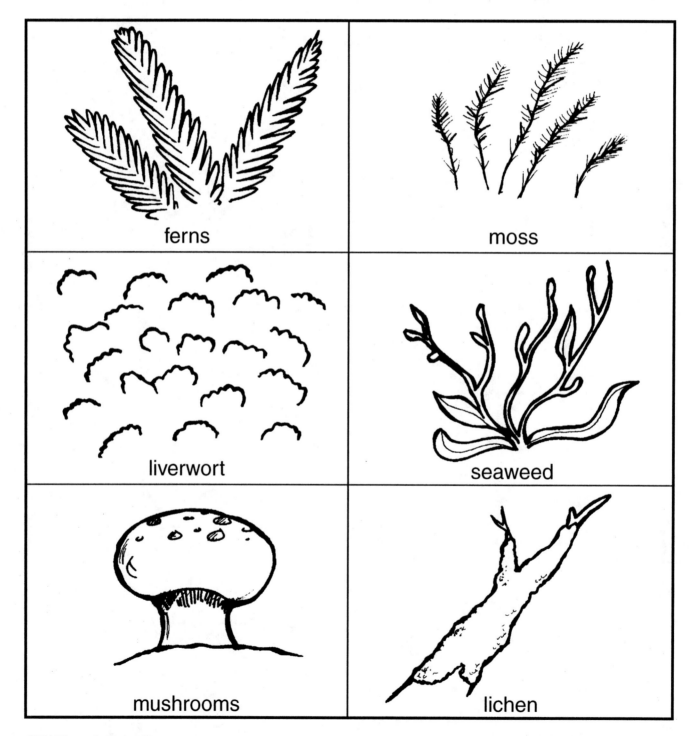

ferns

moss

liverwort

seaweed

mushrooms

lichen

Art and Seeds

These four art projects are fun to do, and all begin with seeds. Choose those that best suit your teaching style and classroom needs.

S Is for Seed

Materials: tagboard or cardboard, scissors, white household glue with a pouring spout, a variety of seeds and dry beans

Directions:

* Review the letter S with the class. Have the children practice writing S's, if necessary.
* Give each child a 6" square (15 cm) piece of tagboard and a glue bottle.
* Direct them to make a letter S onto the tagboard, using the glue.
* Immediately sprinkle seeds and beans over the entire S.
* When the design is dry, cut out around the S (optional).

Extension: Instead of cutting out the S, have the children write some other words or draw pictures onto the tagboard that rhyme with the word seed.

A Seed Bracelet

Materials: Seeds and dry beans, construction paper strips at least 1½ " wide and 7" long (4 cm wide and 18 cm long), paste or glue, stapler

Directions:

* Provide each child with a handful of beans, a construction paper strip, and paste.
* Instruct them to glue seeds and beans onto the construction paper strip.
* When they are dry, make a ring with the strip and staple the two ends together. Make sure you leave enough room for the children to slip their hands through the ring hole.

Seed-Covered Box

Materials: Seeds and dry beans, empty tissue boxes (preferably the cubes) or other small boxes, glue, tempera paint, paint brushes

Directions:

* Paint the boxes with a thick coating of tempera paint and allow plenty of time to dry.
* Glue seed and bean designs on the side faces and tops of the boxes.
* Use to hold pencils, scissors, or other art supplies.

Seed Pin

Materials: Seeds, rolling pin, play clay, cookie cutters, safety pin, poster paint (optional)

Directions:

* Roll out the play clay and cut into desired shapes with cookie cutters.
* Press a variety of seeds onto the surfaces.
* Press a safety pin into the back of the piece. (Make sure the pin opens out.)
* Let dry. Paint, if desired.

Note: If the use of safety pins is inappropriate for your class, make small paperweights instead. Simply follow the directions above and omit the safety pin.

Little Book

3. Root hairs grow from the big root.

4. Roots and root hair spush down into the soil.

5. The seed pushes up through the soil

6. The shoot turns green.

2. A root grows down into the soil.

1. A seed is planted It gets water and sunlight.

How a Seed Grows

by _____

7. Leaves come next.

18

Making a Little Book

Make enough copies of the little book on page 18 for the whole class. Cut out along the solid lines and follow the directions below.

1. Fold the page in half **lengthwise**.

2. Fold in half.

3. Fold in half again.

4. Unfold the paper; you will have eight sections.

5. Fold the page in half along the **width.**

6. Cut or tear along the center crease from the folded edge along the first box.

7. Open up the paper. It should look like diagram 7.

8. Fold it lengthwise once again.

9. Push the end sections together to fold into a little book with four pages.

10. Have the children color the pictures. Let them take turns reading the book to a partner, an older student, a parent volunteer, or to you. After working with the book for a couple days, they may take it home to read to a family member.

To make a little book without the pattern, start with a clean sheet of drawing paper or typing paper. Follow the directions, beginning with number one above. The children can write their own stories and draw pictures.

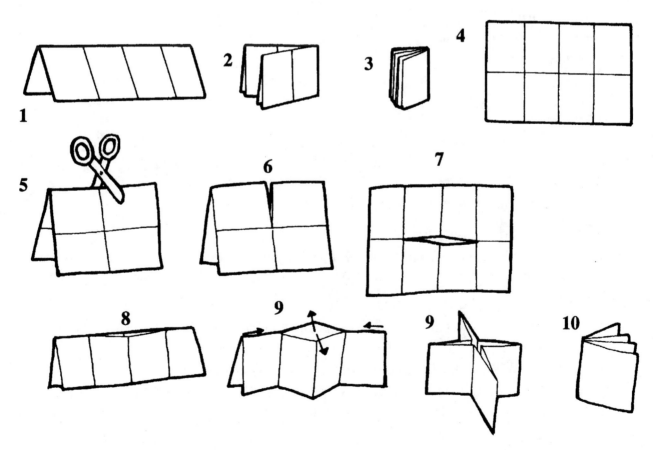

Literature Connections

Use any of the three outstanding literature selections outlined below to introduce, extend, or culminate your studies about seeds.

The Carrot Seed by Ruth Krauss (HarperCollins Children's Books, 1945)
In this 1945 classic a little boy plants a carrot seed and anxiously waits for it to grow.

* **Creative Drama.** Have groups of children enact the book. One of the children acts as the little boy (or change it to a little girl) who plants a seed. Other characters can act as the father, sister, or friend, etc. One at a time, have the characters come up to the boy and say, "I'm afraid it won't come up." The boy may ad lib answers, such as, "Oh, but I think it will."

* **Grow Carrots.** Cut off the top end of a carrot, then place it on a plate layered with pebbles. Add water (check it daily) and watch the carrot grow. The children can record their daily observations.

* **An Innovation.** Write a class innovation of *The Carrot Seed*. Change the main character to a girl who plants a carrot seed. Turn the dialogue into a positive statement such as, "I think it will come up." Change the resulting plant into a miniature carrot.

Pumpkin Pumpkin by Jeanne Titherington (Mulberry Books, 1986)

In the spring Jamie planted a pumpkin seed. All summer long he watched it grow until autumn, when it was perfect for a Halloween Jack-o'-Lantern.

* Make Jack-o'-Lanterns. Carve a pumpkin to make a Jack-o'-Lantern.

Variations:
* With poster paint draw faces on a small pumpkin.
* Glue or pin construction paper eyes, nose, etc., to the pumpkin.
* Use colored tape to make face parts.
* Roasted Seeds. Carve a pumpkin and save the seeds for roasting (see recipe below).
1. Clean the seeds of any pumpkin pulp.
2. Spread the seeds on a cookie sheet.
3. Bake in a 325°F (170°C) oven for 20 minutes or until golden brown.

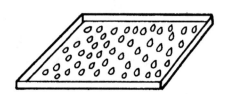

* For more pumpkin activities, see *In a Pumpkin Shell* by Jennifer Storey Gillis (Storey Communications, Inc., 1992).

Cactus Hotel by Brenda Z. Guiberson (Henry Holt and Company, 1991)
This book follows the life of a saguaro cactus from seed through its life in the desert until its death some 200 years later.

* Have the children explain how the cactus seed came to land under the paloverde tree. How else might the seed have been moved there?

* Make a list of some of the animals of the desert. Draw a class mural.

* Talk about who lives in the cactus hotel. Ask the children if a bear would live in a cactus hotel. (The answer is no because bears do not live in the desert.) Continue these questions with different animal names.

Flowers Fruits Seeds

by Jerome Wexler

Summary

Stunningly beautiful color photographs accompany the simply worded text of this beginner's book about plant cycles. The main idea here is that flowers produce fruits which contain seeds.

Now that the children have some knowledge about seeds, they will learn where the seeds come from and how they fit into a plant's life cycle.

Overview of Activities

Setting the Stage

Fruits. Fill a bowl or basket with a variety of fruits. Keep it at your plant center, on your desk, or some other area where the children will be sure to see it.

Favorites. With the children, discuss what kinds of fruits they like to eat. Write each fruit name on a separate index card or pre-cut strip of construction paper. Use these with a pocket chart.

Identification. Have the children identify the fruits in the bowl or basket. On separate index cards write a name card for each fruit. Match the word names to the fruit.

Cutouts. The children can cut out pictures of fruits and flowers from old magazines. Glue the pictures to one large class chart or have each child attach his/her pictures to a paper plate. Extend the activity. Tell the children to write the name of each fruit or flower.

Enjoying the Story

Reading. As you read the text aloud to the children, allow them time to savor the beautiful photographs which accompany the text. How many of the pictures can the children identify?

Unfinished Sentences. Have the children complete the following unfinished sentence: A _____ has flowers. See page 23 for complete directions and some other language development activities.

What's Missing? Place four or five different flowers on a cookie sheet. Have the children sit around you in a circle. Show them the flowers and identify them by name and/or color. Tell the children to close their eyes while you remove one. When you tell them to open their eyes, ask them to identify which one is missing. Continue in the same manner until each flower has been removed at least once.

Alternative: Make poster board flowers, using one of the patterns from the bulletin board (see pages 75 to 79). Attach a small magnet to the back of each flower. Pairs of students can play this game (What's Missing?) together.

Overview of Activities *(cont.)*

Enjoying the Story *(cont.)*

All About Fruits. Send a letter home asking each household for a fruit contribution. (You may want to assign a particular fruit to each family so that you do not end up with only one or two kinds.) A sample letter for you to use can be found on page 26; have the children write in the name of the fruit and a draw a picture, if they can. Collect all the fruits in a large basket or other container. Choose from any of the activities on pages 24 and 25. Follow up with a letter home asking parents to share their child's learning experience. A sample letter is on the bottom of page 26. Space has been provided on the letter to allow the children to draw pictures of their favorite fruits.

Pear Flash Cards. Individuals or pairs can practice matching sets or addition and subtraction problems (see page 28).

Art. There are three different art projects to choose from on page 29.

Fruit Tasting. For four different delicious ways to enjoy fruit, see page 32.

Review. With the students, discuss the main ideas of the book. Some concepts and related activities are provided on pages 33 and 34.

Extending the Story

Big Book Idea. Write a chunk of text on large pieces of construction paper. Give one to each child, pair, or group of children to illustrate. Encourage them to use a variety of materials. Read page 35 for some ideas to get you started.

Science. Learn the plant life cycle: Flowers produce fruit which produce seeds to grow more flowers. Make a life cycle chart. Use one of the procedures on page 36.

More Reading. More resources and literature connections appear on page 38. Use these ideas to extend, reinforce, or introduce your studies of the plant life cycle.

Rhymes and Rhythms. On page 39 you will find some old familiar rhymes and rhythms with a new twist. Patterns for finger puppets to accompany songs and word plays can be found on page 40. Flannel board characters can be created using the apple pattern on page 30.

Bloom Match. Children can match the blooms with the plants pictured on page 41. Make a copy of the page for each pair or small group of children. Cut out on the bold and dashed lines. Direct the children to mix up the cards and place them picture side up on a table or other flat surface. Tell them to place two cards together to make a whole.

Language Development

Develop language and critical thinking skills with the following exercises. They can be used during circle time or completed as small group activities.

Flowers

Establish that many kinds of plants have flowers. Write this language pattern on the chalkboard, chart paper, or overhead projector:

> A _____ has flowers.

Brainstorm with the children some possible names that would appropriately fill in the sentence blank. Record responses on the chalkboard, chart paper, or overhead projector. Practice reading the sentence out loud, supplying a different plant name each time.

Alike and Different

Compare how flowers are alike and different with opposites. (You may need to review opposites with the children.) Prepare a number of sentences to say aloud. See the book *Plants We Know* by O. Irene Sevrey Miner (Children's Press, 1981) for some ideas. Some samples follow:

1. Some flowers are small. Some flowers are _____. (large)

2. Some flowers grow alone. Some flowers grow in ___. (groups)

3. Some flowers smell nice. Some flowers smell _____. (stinky)

4. Some flowers do have petals. Some flowers do _____ have petals. (not)

5. Some flowers grow quickly. Some flowers grow _____. (slowly)

Explore a number of responses for each sentence. Have the children try to compose a sentence along with its opposite.

Circle Time

   * Use circle time to tell a cooperative story about a seedling. Start with one child who says one or two sentences about a seedling. The child on his/her right adds one or two more sentences to the story. Play continues in this manner until all the children have contributed to the tale. For more interest use a prop such as a real seedling. The child who is presently contributing to the story holds the seedling and then passes it on to the next child. You might want to suggest a title or story line before beginning this project. Some examples include, *The Ugly Seedling, How the Seedling Grew as Tall as the School, The Seedling That Grew Two Kinds of Fruit.*

Poetry

Share some poems with the children from the book *Under the Sun and the Moon and Other Poems* by Margaret Wise Brown (Hyperion Books for Children, 1993). Two selections from this book are especially appropriate —"Apple Trees" and "Dream of a Weed." Use the following language pattern with the children and have them supply new rhyming lines:

> Dream of a weed growing from a seed

All About Fruit

The projects outlined below will help the children learn all about fruit. In addition, the activities develop critical thinking skills, review and reinforce math concepts and reading skills, and encourage creativity. Choose those which best suit your classroom objectives and teaching style.

* Have the students identify each fruit. Write the names on separate index cards; display the fruits with their word names on a table. Remove the word names. Direct the children to match the name with the corresponding fruit.

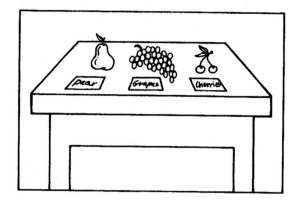

* In circle time talk about some fruit products. For example, ask what kinds of foods can be made with apples (applesauce, apple cake, apple fritters, apple juice, etc.) or grapes (raisins, juice, wine, etc.).

* Use circle time to talk about some words that rhyme with berry. Record the responses on chart paper. Make up two-line rhyming poems. See the example that follows.

> He bit into a berry
>
> But he thought it was
> a cherry!

* Estimate how many seeds are in a fruit. Let each child write his/her number on a sticky note. Have the children make a graph by placing all the one's in a column, the two's in the next column, etc., on the chalkboard or a wall where the notes will adhere. Then open the fruit and count the number of seeds.

* Eat some seeds. Try roasted pumpkin seeds (for a simple recipe see page 20), sunflower seeds, or sesame seeds. Pop some popcorn (more popcorn ideas appear on the Popcorn Page, page 27).

* Use the seeds to make math flash cards. Glue a different number of seeds to each index card. Write the numeral on the back of the card. Children can practice counting by themselves or with a partner. (Patterns for pear flash cards can be found on page 28. The fruit patterns on pages 30 and 31 may also be used to make flash cards.)

* A variation on the above idea is to have the children make seed numerals. Let them choose a numeral or assign one that you are studying, for example, the numeral six. Give each child a large index card to draw a six on. Glue seeds to the outline of the six. Practice writing sixes all around the seeded six.

All About Fruit *(cont.)*

* Cut open a fruit. Count the seeds. Practice writing that number (if there are eight seeds, write the number eight). Draw or make physical sets of that number (e.g., draw eight flowers or make a set of eight blocks).

* Save the seeds from many fruits. Compare them. How do they feel? Which is the largest? Which is the smallest? What colors are they? Which fruit had the most seeds? Which fruit had the least amount of seeds?

* You will need a number of seeds and about six clean, empty yogurt cups with lids (or plastic margarine cups) for this project.

1. Fill each cup with a different number of seeds. Have the children arrange the cups in order of weight from heaviest to lightest or from lightest to heaviest.

2. Provide the child with an empty cup and a handful of dried beans. Have him/her choose one of the filled cups. Direct the child to put enough beans in the empty cup so that it weighs the same as the filled one.

* Observe a fruit that has been cut open. Talk about the design that is formed by the seeds inside the pulp. Apples have a star; do other fruits? Direct the children to draw a picture of a cut-open fruit along with its seed pattern. Another option is to have them glue a number of seeds into the correct pattern on the drawn fruit. To help the children visualize the inside section of a fruit, show the children the book *Fruit* by Gallimard Jeunesse (Scholastic, 1989). It has overlay pages and cutaway drawings of a variety of fruits. Also, *What's Inside? Plants* (Dorling Kindersley, Inc., 1992) provides inside and outside pictures of a number of plants.

* Use the cut fruit to make fruit prints. For directions for fruit prints and two other art projects see page 29.

* Cut fruit open and give each child a taste. If you prefer, use the cut fruit to make fruit salad. Some easy recipes appear on page 32.

* Have a fruit tasting party to which everyone contributes a food item made with fruit-fruited yogurt, pumpkin bread, blueberry pancakes, raisin cookies, etc. Divide the food into tiny bites so everyone can get a taste of the different foods. During circle time have the children tell which ones were their favorites and why.

Family Letters

Use the first letter to gather fruits for a fruit tasting party. Follow up with a letter asking parents to become involved with their children.

Dear Family,

(Name)_____ is learning all about fruit. On (day)

_____ (date) _____ there will be a fruit

tasting event in class. Please send the following fruit to school with your

child on that day.

Fruit Name

Thank you for your cooperation.

Sincerely yours,

_____

(Teacher Signature)

Dear Family,

Today in school we had a fruit tasting party. Ask your child to tell you all

about it. Here is a picture of his/her favorite fruit.

Sincerely yours,

_____

(Teacher Signature)

Popcorn Page

Popcorn is an especially enjoyable seed to work with. Below are a number of learning activities for you to choose from.

Literature

* As an introduction read aloud *The Popcorn Book* by Tomie dePaola or *Corn Is Maize* by Aliki. (See bibliography on page 80.)

Math

* Give each pair of children a handful of popcorn seeds. Direct them to make a set of seven seeds, five seeds, ten seeds.

* Have the children model math problems with the popcorn seeds. For the problem 7-3, the children will make a set of seven seeds and physically remove three. Then they will count the remaining seeds.

* Give each pair a paper plate. Have them use the seeds to illustrate greater than and fewer than. Tell the children to draw a line down the center of the plate. On one side of the line, make a set of five popcorn seeds. On the other side of the line make a set of two popcorn seeds. Which side has more seeds? Which side has fewer? Repeat the process with other sets.

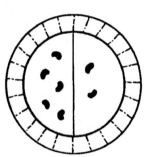

Science

* Plant some popcorn. Fill each foam cup three-fourths full with potting soil. With the thumb make a hole in the center of the soil. Add water and then the seed. Cover with more soil. Observe daily for changes. On a class chart record changes with drawings and stories. (Be sure to continue to water seeds when necessary.)

* Before popping some popcorn have the children estimate how much popcorn the unpopped kernels will make. Will the pan be full, half full, etc.? Sample the popped corn; save some of it for art projects.

* Make a class chart of some other corn products—cornbread, caramel corn, corn nuts, etc. Have a corn product tasting party. (**Note:** Check for any allergies to corn.) Let the children vote on their favorites.

* Use the same corn products from the above activity to compare how each one tastes, looks, and smells.

Art

* Color the unpopped popcorn with food coloring. Squeeze a few drops of coloring into a resealable plastic bag. Add a handful of popcorn and squish the coloring around until it is evenly spread. Allow to dry inside the bag for at least 24 hours. Make as many colors as you will need. Colored seeds can be used for mosaics.

* Glue clusters of popped popcorn onto construction paper to make flowers. Add crayon or construction paper leaves and stems.

For more popcorn activities see Teacher Created Material's #263 *Popcorn—A Thematic Unit.*

Pear Flash Cards

Game I Make six copies of this page for each child. Draw one to twelve seeds on each set of cards. Have the children match the sets.

Game II Make as many copies of this page as you will need. Write a different addition or subtraction problem on each pear. Write the corresponding answers on a second set of pear cards.

Note: The fruit patterns from pages 30 and 31 may also be used for these activities. For more durability, glue the cards to tagboard and laminate. Write on the laminated cards with wipe-off pens. Store all cards in a manila envelope.

You may also want to use these patterns for the 3-D art project on the next page.

Fruit and Art

Fruit Prints

Materials: Paper plates, thick liquid tempera paints, drawing paper or white construction paper, variety of fruits (those with hard surfaces, such as apples, grapefruits, and oranges work best), knife

Directions:

* With the knife, cut the fruits in halves or quarters.
* Pour a different color of liquid tempera paint on each plate.
* Show the children how to dip the cut surface of the fruit into the paint and press it onto the drawing paper. Depending on how much paint is on the fruit, two or more prints may be made from one dipping.
* Repeat the process with other fruits and colors on the same page.
* When the paint is dry have the children add details such as seeds.

3-D Fruit

Materials: Copies of patterns on pages 30 and 31, construction paper, scissors, old newspapers or tissue, stapler, tempera paint or marking pens, string or yarn

Directions:

* On colored construction paper make enough copies of the fruit patterns for the class. You will need two copies of a fruit to make these three-dimensional.
* Give a different fruit to each child and have him/her cut out both pattern pieces.
* With tempera paint or marking pens, add details (seeds, rind, etc.)
* Place both pattern pieces together and staple about two-thirds of the way around them leaving a space large enough for the children to stuff in wads of newspaper or tissue.
* After the newspaper or tissue has been added, staple the hole shut.
* To display the 3-D art work, staple a long piece of string or yarn to the fruit piece and hang it from a ceiling hook.

Outside Inside

Materials: Drawing paper, crayons, fruit (one whole and one cut section)

Directions:

* Display a whole piece of fruit and a section of the same fruit.
* Show the children how to fold the drawing paper in half like a greeting card.
* With crayons have them draw the whole fruit on the paper. Label it outside.
* Open up the folded paper and draw a picture of the inside of the fruit. Label it inside.

Note: A great resource for this activity is the book *What's Inside? Plants* (Dorling Kindersley, Inc., 1992)

Fruit Patterns

* For directions see page 29

30

Fruit Patterns *(cont.)*

* For directions see page 29.

Fruit Recipes

Fruit Kabobs

Ingredients: Chunks of fruit (you may want to cut these ahead of time), maraschino cherries for garnish

Equipment: Wood skewers (available at grocery and party supply stores), knife (if you are cutting the fruit during class)

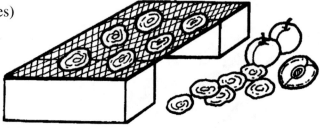

Directions:
* Alternate chunks of fruit on each skewer, for example, pineapple, banana, apple, orange, strawberry, and a cherry garnish.

Tropical Fruit Salad

Ingredients: Kiwi fruit, mango, pineapple, guava, packaged shredded coconut

Equipment: Bowl, spoon for stirring and serving, knife, plastic cups and spoons
Directions:
* Cut up the fruits.
* Mix together in a bowl.
* Serve in plastic cups. Top with a sprinkle of shredded coconut.

Berry Good Dessert

Ingredients: An assortment of berries (strawberries, blueberries, blackberries, etc.), prepared vanilla pudding, pound cake, whipped cream (optional)
Equipment: Knife, spoons, paper plates, plastic forks or spoons

Directions:
* Clean the berries and mix together (whole or cut up) in a bowl.
* Slice the pound cake. Place one slice on each plate.
* Spread a layer of pudding on the cake.
* Sprinkle with the berries. Top with whipped cream, if desired.

Dried Peaches

Ingredients: Peaches (peeled, cored, and cut in slices)
Equipment: Clean mesh screen, bricks, cheesecloth

Directions:
* Suspend the mesh screen on the bricks.
* Place the peach slices on the screen and cover with cheesecloth.
* Allow plenty of time to dry (minimum of one day). Fruit is done when it feels leathery but is still moist inside.

Concepts

On this page and the next you will find a number of concepts that you may want to reinforce. Math, science. reading, and art are incorporated into the suggested activities. For easy reference, sample answers appear in parentheses.

1. **Concept:** Many kinds of plants have flowers.

    Activities:

    * Name some plants that have flowers. (dahlia, tulip, tree, pussy willow, vines, cactus, tomatoes, grasses, weeds, house plants, garden plants, etc.)
    * Draw or cut out pictures of plants from catalogs and magazines. Label with names.
    * Go on a walking field trip. Have the children identify plants with flowers.

2. **Concept:** Flowers are special parts of plants.

    Activities:

    * Ask, "What do flowers do?" (They produce fruits that contain seeds.)
    * Look at famous paintings of flowers such as *"Oriental Poppies"* by Georgia O'Keeffe or "Irises" by Vincent Van Gogh. Have the children describe how the pictures make them feel.
    * Follow up by having the children paint flowers in the same styles as famous artists. If you want the children to draw an O'Keeffe flower, for instance, show them how to use the whole page for their drawings. If you choose an Impressionist artist such as Van Gogh, use this method:

        1. Have the children use cotton swabs instead of paint brushes.
        2. Dip the swab into a color of liquid paint and make dabs onto the drawing paper.
        3. Continue in the same manner until the flower is complete.
        4. Use a different swab for each color.

3. **Concept:** Flowers are alike and different.

    Activities:

    * Discuss how flowers are alike and different. (Some are small and some are large; some have petals and some do not; some are colorful and some are not; some grow alone and others grow in groups; some smell nice and some smell unpleasant.)
    * Compare a cactus flower with a rose, for example. Make a class chart of how they are alike and how they are different. Variation: Discuss with children whether the flowers are large or small, whether they have petals, whether they smell nice, etc.

4. **Concept**: In general, a flower's function is to produce fruit which contains seeds.

    Activities:

    * Cut open a number of fruits; find the seeds.
    * Draw cutaway pictures of fruit and their seeds. With poster paints paint a cutaway picture. When it is dry, glue some real seeds to the inside section.

Concepts *(cont.)*

5. **Concept:** There are many kinds of fruits.

   Activities:

   * Discuss the different kinds. (Some are soft and juicy and good to eat raw; some are hard; some taste bad; some have sharp spines, hair, or tough skin; some are thin; some are poisonous.)

   * Observe a number of real fruits. Discuss to which of the above mentioned categories they belong.

   * Group the children. Give each group a number of real fruits. Tell them to classify the fruits any way they would like (texture, color, size, etc.). One group at a time, have them explain how they classified the fruits.

   * Write a class book about fruit.

   1. Label each page with a one-sentence text such as, "Some fruits are soft and juicy" or "Some fruits have thin skin."

      2. Give one page to each group of children.

      3. Have the children draw illustrations to go with the text.

      4. Collect all the finished pages and staple along one side to make a class book.

6. Concept: The purpose of fruits is to protect the seeds inside them.

   Activities:

   * Cut open a piece of fruit. Observe how the seeds are surrounded by pulp.

   * Make a fruit with seeds. You will need a break apart plastic egg, cotton balls, and large beans (limas, pinto, kidney, etc.).

      1. Wrap the seeds (beans) with the cotton.

      2. Stuff them into the plastic egg cup. Add more cotton.

      3. Close up the cup. Have the children open the cup and find the protected seeds.

7. **Concept:** There are many kinds of seeds.

   Activities:

   * Brainstorm a list of the different kinds. (Some are large; some are small; some are smooth; some are rough; some are good to eat; some are poisonous.)

   * Compare seeds from a number of different fruits. Group the smooth ones, the small ones, the large ones, etc.

   * Talk about some seeds that are edible. Eat some seeds—-sunflower seeds, pomegranate seeds, and pumpkin seeds are popular. (Make roasted pumpkin seeds. See page 20 for an easy recipe.)

8. **Concept:** In general, the purpose of a seed is to grow a new plant.

   Activities:

   * Grow some seeds (see page 10 for seed-growing ideas).

   * Make a plant life cycle chart (directions are on page 36).

Big Book Illustrations

Read through the list of materials below and collect as many as possible for the children to use in making Big Book Illustrations that are truly unique. Send a note home asking for donations of these supplies. Others can be obtained from hardware stores or department stores, often for free. Some art ideas to get you started can be found after the list of materials.

Materials:

aluminum foil	fabric scraps	yarn and colored string
lace or other trim	colored plastic wrap	colored art tissue
paint chip samples	craft sticks	paper plates
crepe paper	cotton puffs	colored book tape
twigs	real flowers /plants	sequins or glitter
ice cream sticks	old magazines	pipe cleaners
felt	sandpaper	newspaper
paper bags	toothpicks	straws
wallpaper samples	popped popcorn	colored glue
shredded paper	cotton swabs	

How to Make

Flowers: * Use actual flowers or flower parts. * Cut colored art tissue paper into small squares or shapes; apply layer by layer to the paper with watered-down liquid white glue. * Fabric pieces, felt, and wallpaper samples can be cut into flower shapes. * Draw a flower outline with liquid white glue. Sprinkle sequins or glitter onto the glue lines. * To make a pussy willow, draw or paint branches; attach cotton puff flowers. * Popped popcorn can be used for blossoms; draw green leaves around the flower.

Trees: * Twigs and small branches of trees will work just fine here. * Craft sticks or ice cream sticks can be painted with brown marking pen or tempera paint. * Cut sandpaper, felt, or newspaper for tree trunks and branches. * Use toothpicks to outline tree trunks or as branches.

Fruits: * Draw and color a picture of a fruit or cut out a shape from colored construction paper. * Glue some actual fruit seeds to the picture. * With colored liquid glue, draw the outline of a fruit. When the glue is dry, color the inside of the space with art chalk.

Cactus: * Cut out a sandpaper shape (see page 37 for a cactus pattern). Color the cactus leaves with green chalk. Glue on toothpicks for spines. * With white chalk draw a cactus on green or tan construction paper. Cut off the tips of cotton swabs and glue them to the cactus.

Ground: * Cut out sandpaper for the ground; glue to paper. * Use shredded paper for grass. * Colored plastic wrap can be used for grass or water.

All: * Find and cut out pictures from old magazines and newspapers. Paste or glue to the page. * Enhance cut-outs by outlining each picture with black marker or crayon. * Add details such as real seeds or twigs to the pictures. * Add powdered tempera color to liquid white glue; mix thoroughly. Draw a thick outline of a particular flower, tree, or other plant. When it dries it will have a raised surface. Color the inside of the shape with art chalk.

Life Cycle Charts

Follow the directions below to make a plant life cycle chart. A variation of the idea and instructions for a triangle chart are also provided.

Paper Plate Chart

Materials: Paper plates, old magazines (especially ones that include pictures of nature like *Better Homes and Gardens, Sunset,* and *National Geographic)* or seed packets, glue, scissors, black crayons

Directions:

* Cut out one picture each of flowers, fruits, and seeds. Glue the three pictures to the paper plate—the fruit on top, flowers on the lower left, the seeds on the lower right.
* Draw lines between the pictures.
* Discuss each picture and the sequence of the plant life cycle.
* Write simple sentences next to each picture. (Many plants have flowers. Flowers make fruit. Fruits have seeds to grow more plants.)

Variation:

* You will need three paper plates for one chart.
* Cut out pictures of flowers, fruits, and seeds.
* Paste a number of flower pictures to one plate, fruit pictures to another plate, and seed pictures to a third plate.
* Attach the three plates to a classroom wall—the fruit pictures on top, the seed pictures to the right, the flowers to the left.
* Connect the three paper plates with lengths of craft yarn (see diagram).

Triangle Chart

Materials: Large piece of poster board or tagboard, scissors, old magazines, glue

Directions:

* Cut a large sheet of poster board or tagboard into a triangle shape.
* Instruct the children to cut out pictures of flowers, fruits, and seeds from old magazines.
* Have them glue the fruit pictures at the top of the triangle, the flower pictures in the left angle, and the seed pictures in the right angle.
* Review and identify the steps in the plant life cycle.

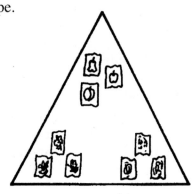

Cactus Pattern

* See page 35 for suggested uses.

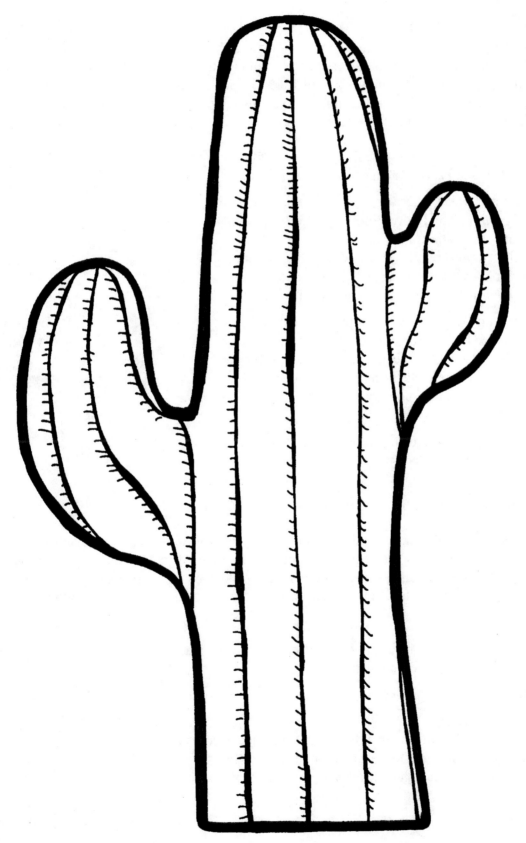

Literature Connections

Introduce, reinforce, or extend plant cycle concepts with either of these two literature selections.

Johnny Appleseed by Steven Kellogg (Morrow, 1988)

In this lively retelling of the saga of John Chapman—a.k.a. Johnny Appleseed—we learn of one man's crusade to clear the land and plant apple trees for the coming settlers. Johnny's journey took him across Ohio and through Indiana where he died in 1845. He led a simple life and in the process became a great American hero. Whimsical illustrations (also by the author Steven Kellogg) add to the feeling of an earlier historical era.

* **Apples.** Cut apples into fourths. Give children apple slices and let them eat the apple pieces while you read aloud a story about Johnny Appleseed.

* **Other Versions.** Read other versions about this folk hero. In *Johnny Appleseed* by Reeve Lindbergh (Little, Brown and Company, 1990) the author relays the story in verse. (Colorful illustrations reminiscent of Grandma Moses make this book a visual feast as well. Aliki also has an enjoyable *Johnny Appleseed* (Prentice-Hall, 1963).

* **Creative Drama.** The children can pretend they are Johnny Appleseed. For props use a pot with a handle, a paper sack full of seeds (or beans), and a small plastic shovel. Let the children take turns enacting Johnny as he plants seeds all around the country.

* **Time Line.** Make a time line of events in the Johnny Appleseed story. Write each event on a separate index card. With clothespins attach them in correct chronological order on a clothesline.

Fruit & Vegetable Man by Roni Schotter (Little, Brown and Company, 1993)

For nearly fifty years Ruby Rubenstein jumped out of bed every morning, anxious to get to his store. He bought only the freshest fruits and vegetables, and his customers depended on him. Sun Ho, a neighborhood boy, enjoyed watching Ruby work his magic and soon he began learning the business. One day Ruby became ill. Sun Ho and his family went to the rescue and the colorful neighborhood business lived on.

* **Taste!** Ruby liked to give his customers a taste of his fruits and vegetables. Make a tray of fruits and vegetables for the children to sample.

* **Field Trip.** Visit a local produce store. Observe how the fruits and vegetables are arranged on the shelves.

* **Drawing.** Cut 8" (20 cm) squares out of drawing paper. Fold each piece in half diagonally and cut to make two triangles. Give each child a triangle. Instruct them to draw and color an arrangement of fruit and vegetables that Ruby might have made.

Rhymes and Rhythms

Apple Tree

Verse I

Way up high in an apple tree
Ten red apples smiled at me.
I shook that tree as hard as I could.
Down came one apple
Yum! Was it good!

Verse II

Way up high in an apple tree.
Nine red apples smiled at me.
I shook that tree as hard as I could.
Down came one apple
Yum! Was it good!

* Continue counting backwards on each subsequent verse.
* Substitute another fruit for apples—peaches, oranges, cherries, etc.
* Create flannel board characters, using the apple pattern on page 30. Make ten apples. Take one away on each subsequent verse.

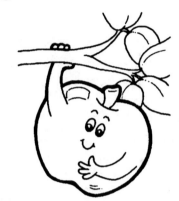

How Is Seedling?

To the tune of *"Where Is Thumbkin?"*

* Listen to "Where Is Thumbkin?" on cassette—*Wee Sing Nursery Rhymes & Lullabies* published by Price Stern Sloan.
* Use the seedling finger puppets on page 40. Create finger movements using the seedling finger puppets on page 40.

How is seedling? How is seedling? I am growing. I am growing. How are you today, seed? Growing quickly each day. Bye for now. Bye for now.

How is seedling? How is seedling? I grew roots. I grew roots. How are you today, seed? Growing more roots daily. Bye for now. Bye for now.

How is seedling? How is seedling? I grew shoots. I grew shoots. How are you today, seed? Growing more shoots daily. Bye for now. Bye for now.

How is seedling? How is seedling? I grew leaves. I grew leaves. Now I am a big plant. Now I am a big plant. Bye for now. Bye for now.

Coconuts

Five brown coconuts sitting in a tree
One for you and four for me.
Or three for you and two for me.

* Continue the verses, using any combination that makes five.
* Change the number of coconuts in the first verse and make appropriate changes in subsequent verses.

Seedling Finger Puppets

Have the children color, cut out, and wear these finger puppets while singing "How Is Seedling?" See page 39 for words to the verses.

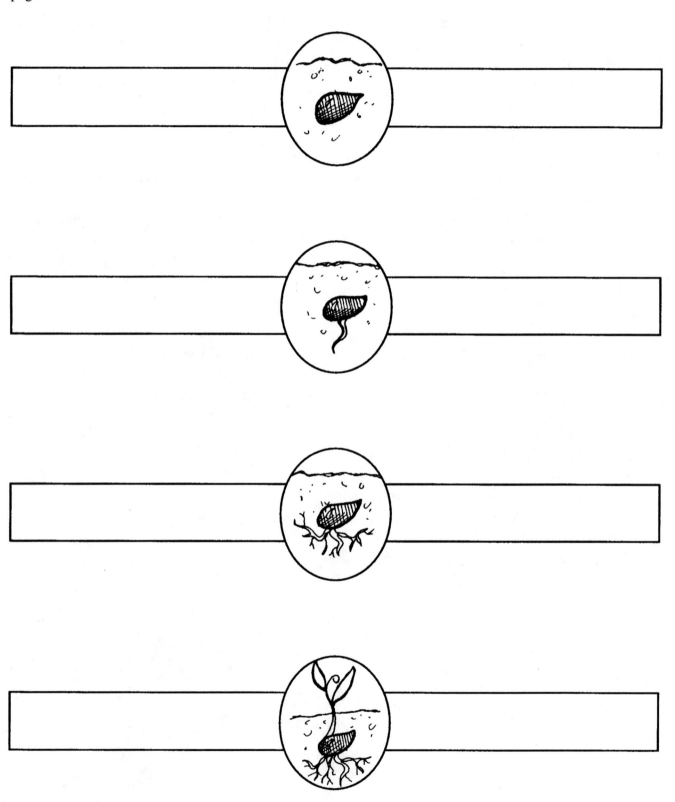

Bloom Match

* For directions see page 22.

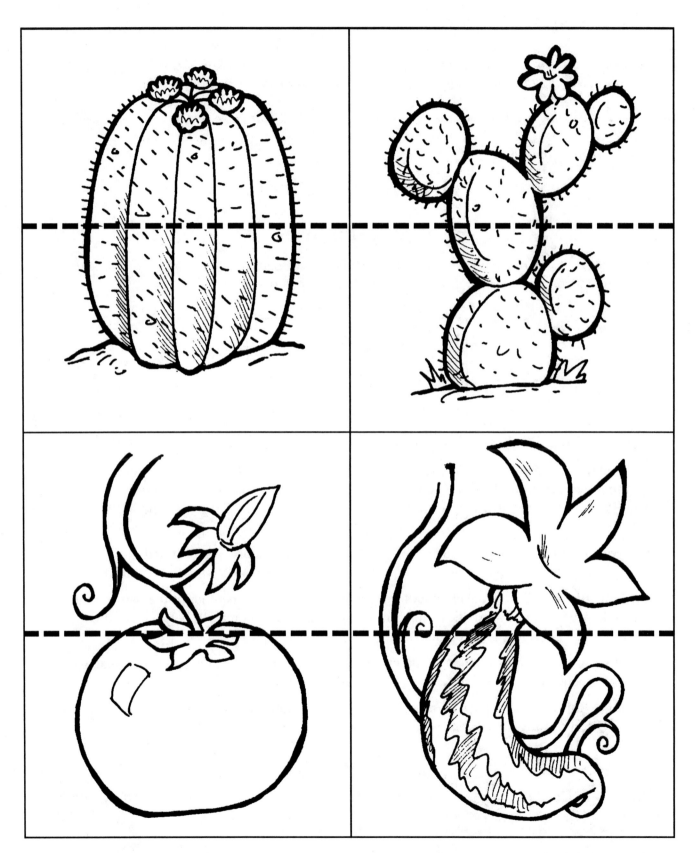

Planting a Rainbow

by Lois Ehlert

Summary

In the fall a child and mother buy bulbs and plant them in the ground. During the winter they order seeds from catalogs. They wait for spring when the bulbs sprout. Then they buy and plant seedlings. All summer long they watch their garden grow and grow into a colorful display of flowers. They pick the flowers and bring them home, knowing that next year they will grow another rainbow.

The simple story line, bright colors, and book-within-a-book format make this a most appealing book for children of all ages. It is sure to capture the imaginations of your youngsters and make them eager to plant gardens of their own.

Overview of Activities

Setting the Stage

Bulletin Board. Construct the Rainbow of Flowers Bulletin Board on pages 75 to 79. Call attention to the six different colors of flowers displayed on the bulletin board.

Review Colors. Review the six colors contained in the bulletin board display. Read aloud the book *Mouse Paint* by Ellen Stoll Walsh (Harcourt Brace Jovanovich, 1989). Discuss how various colors are formed. Perform a color experiment with food coloring and water. See pages 44 and 45 for more color projects.

Introduction. Introduce the topic of rainbows with the charming story of a bear and his adventures with a rainbow. This book is *A Rainbow of My Own* by Don Freeman (Viking Press, 1966).

Reading Readiness. Prepare the children for *Planting a Rainbow* with either of the two activities described on page 46. Both activities emphasize patterns and colors and will help the children recognize various configurations (outlines).

Yarn Rainbow. Make a yarn rainbow with craft yarn, glue, and construction paper. See page 47 for complete instructions, along with directions for two other art projects.

An Outdoor Rainbow. Children can observe a rainbow firsthand with this easy demonstration (see page 49). Directions for other science projects are also provided on that page.

Enjoying the Story

Reading. Read aloud *Planting a Rainbow*. Allow the children plenty of time to savor the colorful collage of flowers on every page.

Overview of Activities *(cont.)*

Enjoying the Story *(cont.)*

Thinking Skills. Develop thinking skills with the two strategies described on page 50. The circle time activity can be used to assess the children's knowledge of story events while the second activity emphasizes the comprehension skill of telling what happens next.

Circle Time. Different techniques to use during circle time are outlined on page 51. All of them will help reinforce the text and content of *Planting a Rainbow*.

Bulb Matching. In this cut-and-paste activity on page 52 the children will match bulb shapes. The patterns can also be used with the second activity on page 46.

Writing and Poetry. On page 53 are a number of writing projects from which to choose. Suggested literature connections are also mentioned.

Math Connections. Three math lessons, all based on the text of *Planting a Rainbow,* are provided for you on page 54. Use beans or seeds for counters.

Extending the Story

Big Book. Culminate your studies of plants with a rainbow Big Book. On page 55 there are two different book formats from which to choose. The overlapping book is based on the last pages of *Planting a Rainbow*—only strips of color show until the pages are turned to reveal the flowers. One or two children can work together to make an overlapping book.

The second format is based on the same overlapping design, but each pair or group of children gets a page to work on together. When all the pages are completed, align them on the left side. Staple together and display at your Reading Center or classroom library.

Art Ideas. Different methods of constructing flowers for a Big Book can be seen on page 56. Some flower patterns are on page 57.

Literature Connections. Extend your study of plants with either of the two resources on page 58.

* *Growing Vegetable Soup* is another Lois Ehlert book that is every bit as colorful and engaging as *Planting a Rainbow*. Have the children compare the two stories.
* *Miss Rumphius* by Barbara Cooney tells the story of a librarian who wants to make the world a better place. After traveling the world she decides to plant lupines.

Color Projects

Any of the following projects can be employed to extend and reinforce concepts about colors.

Another Read Aloud

A delightful way to introduce the topic of rainbows is through the book *A Rainbow of My Own* by Don Freeman (Viking Press, 1966). Have children write or draw pictures of their own rainbow adventure. Arrange all the stories and drawings in a quilt pattern on a classroom wall. Make a banner or headline that says Our Rainbow Stories.

Read aloud the book *Mouse Paint* by Ellen Stoll Walsh (Harcourt Brace Jovanovich, 1989). In this engaging tale about three mice and some cans of paint, the children will see how the different colors are formed. Extend the reading with the color experiment that follows. (For more activities based on *Mouse Paint* see Teacher Created Resources #346 *Connecting Art and Literature.*)

Color Experiment

Materials: Clear plastic cups or baby food jars, water, food coloring, plastic spoons or craft sticks

Procedure:

* Fill a cup or jar half full of water.
* Before adding two drops of red food coloring to the water have the children predict what will happen.
* Then have the children predict what will happen if yellow food coloring is added to the red water.
* Add two drops of yellow food coloring.
* Follow the same procedure for blue and yellow and for red and blue.
* Allow time for the children to work in pairs and experiment on their own.
* Watercolors may be used instead of food coloring.

Rainbow

Write the word rainbow using a different crayon for each letter in the word. Then draw a red contour line around the whole word. Outline that contour with orange, then yellow, blue, green and violet. (See diagram.)

A Green Day

During your study of colors, choose a day to be Green Day. Do one or more of the following activities.

* Tell the children to wear something green to school.
* Have them do all written work with green crayons or pencils.
* Draw pictures of things that are green. Use green paint or crayons.
* Identify all the green things in the classroom.
* Eat something green—pears, lettuce, celery, peas, etc.
* Make green gelatin or pistachio pudding. Drink a lime beverage.

These same ideas can be applied for a Red Day or any other color that you choose.

Variation: Declare a Green Week or Red Week. Employ the same activities outlined above throughout the whole week.

Color Projects *(cont.)*

Color Names

* * Label objects in the classroom with their color names. After a specific length of time, remove the color name tags and distribute them to the children. In turn the children can match an item with its color name.

* * Practice writing the color names. For example, have the children write the word blue three times in blue crayon.

* * Use the color names in a given language pattern. Try this example: A _____ is blue.
  Direct the children to copy the words onto a sheet of paper and supply a proper response (a word or a picture) to complete the sentence.

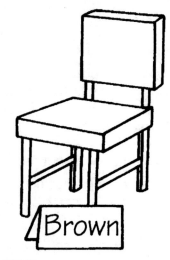

Who Said Red?

Read aloud the book *Who Said Red?* by Mary Serfozo (Aladdin Books, 1992).

The children will enjoy this story poem about the color red. Along the way they meet "blue jean blue," "yellow, bright and mellow. . . ," and on through purple, brown, orange, pink, and black. Impressionistic watercolors enhance this engaging concept book.

* * Pair the children and have them enact a conversation similar to one in the book. One student chooses a color and says, "Who says red?" The other partner responds, "I said red. Very berry, cherry red," or any other red fruits or vegetables they want to name. Another sample conversation:

  "Who says blue?"
  "I say blue. As deep as a blueberry blue."

Have the children change roles. If they cannot think of a vegetable or fruit, have them name another object that is that color.

Color Poems

Write some color poems. Introduce the idea with readings from the classic color book *Hailstones and Halibut Bones* by Mary O'Neill (Delacorte Press, 1961). All the poems but the last one in the book begin with "What Is _____?" Have the children use that same language pattern to begin their own color poems. They may write or dictate the poems and draw illustrations.

Reading Readiness

Here are two activities that will help prepare the children for more formal reading lessons. Enlist parents to donate any items required for these projects or ask them to help prepare any of the necessary patterns and shapes.

Patterns

Materials: Two dozen tongue depressors or clean craft sticks, red, orange, yellow, green, blue, and violet tempera paint, paintbrushes, two paper egg cartons

Directions:

* Paint the top half of four tongue depressors with the red tempera paint.
* Push the unpainted bottom portion of each stick into an egg cup bottom (see diagram) to dry.

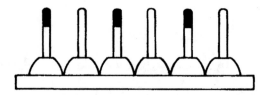

* Paint the remaining tongue depressors in the same manner, using the other five colors.

Game:

* Give each child half of the colored tongue depressors (two of each color). Make a pattern with any four of the sticks. Tell the child to duplicate the pattern with his/her sticks.
* Children can be paired to complete this activity once they are familiar with the process.

Another Game:

* Distribute all the colored tongue depressors. Tell all the greens to stand, all the reds to wave the sticks, all the blues to come to the front of the group, etc.

Bulb Shapes

Materials: Red, yellow, blue, and green construction paper, scissors, patterns from Bulb Matching on page 52

Directions:

* Use the patterns from the Bulb Matching page to make four of each bulb in each of the four colors, i.e., four red irises, four yellow irises, four blue irises, and four green irises.

Game:

* Divide the bulbs evenly according to shape and color so that both you and the child have identical sets.
* Make a repeating series with the bulbs, leaving off the last one in the series.
* Instruct the child to complete the series with one of his bulbs.
* Once the children are familiar with the process, they can be paired to play the game together.

Variation: Make felt figures, using the bulb patterns on page 52. On a flannel board follow the same procedure for the game outlined above.

Rainbow Art

Yarn Rainbow

Materials: Craft yarn in red, orange, yellow, green, blue, and violet, paste or glue, scissors, white construction paper

Directions:

* Cut lengths of yarn—one of each color—for every child.
* Direct the child to spread a line of paste or glue near the top of the construction paper.
* Have the child place and press the red yarn onto the glue line.
* Continue in the same manner until all six colors of the rainbow are represented.
* Children may add a sky with sun and/or clouds if they would like.

Rainbow Flowers

Materials: Flower pattern from page 48 (red, orange, yellow, green, blue, and violet crayons), green craft yarn (or regular yarn), scissors, paste or glue

Directions:

* Make enough copies of the flower pattern for your class.
* Tell the children to color each petal a different color of the rainbow.
* Color the leaves green.
* Cut a length of yarn for the stem and glue the yarn to the page.

Sparkling Flower Mural

Materials: Salt, dry tempera paint (red, orange, yellow, green, blue, violet), plastic margarine cups with lids, glue, butcher paper, masking tape

Directions:

* Mix equal amounts of salt and dry tempera paint in a plastic cup. Cover with the lid and shake carefully to mix.
* Prepare all six colors in the same manner.
* Spread the butcher paper across a long table.
* Have the children dribble glue to make flower shapes on the butcher paper.
* Sprinkle the salt/tempera paint mixture over the glue outline.
* When the glue dries, gently shake off the excess coloring.
* Hang up the mural for all to enjoy.

Rainbow Flowers *(cont.)*

* See page 47 for complete directions on using this page.

48

Science Activities

Making a Rainbow

Materials: Glass of water, sunlight

Procedure:

* Hold the glass of water in the sunlight. Keep moving it around until a rainbow of colors can be seen.

Variation:

* Use a prism to make a rainbow. Hold it up to the sunlight until a rainbow appears on the wall or ceiling.

An Outdoor Rainbow

Materials: A bright, sunny day, garden hose with adjustable nozzle

Procedure:

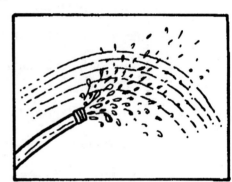

* This works best in late afternoon when the sun is more than halfway down from overhead.
* Adjust the nozzle hose to a fine spray.
* Standing with your back to the sun, direct the spray toward the east at a high angle.
* Observe the rainbow within the mist.

A Portable Garden

Materials: three heavy-duty cardboard boxes, utility knife, heavy-duty plastic garbage bags, potting soil bulbs, seeds and seedlings, spoons, water

Procedure:

* With the utility knife, trim the sides of each box to a height of 6" (15 cm).
* Line the cardboard boxes with plastic garbage bags (you may have to cut them to fit).
* Label one box BULBS, one box SEEDS, one box SEEDLINGS.
* Pour potting soil into each box. Make holes for planting with the hand or a spoon.
* Plant all bulbs, seeds, and seedlings in their corresponding boxes. Add water.
* Observe and record the growth changes over a period of time. (See page 11.)
* The plant boxes can be moved as needed. Compare the growth among the three types of plants.

Habitats

Through books, films, or field trips explore other environments in which plants grow. Some suggestions follow. (You may want to read *Plants That Never Ever Bloom* by Ruth Heller (Grosset & Dunlap, 1984) for background information.

* **Desert.** Observe some cacti. How do they differ from a daisy or ivy? Describe the environment in which they grow. Draw desert scenes with a variety of cactus plants.
* **Ocean.** Visit an aquarium or the ocean. Look for and identify seaweed and kelp. Have the children touch the plants Pand describe how they feel.
* **Forest.** Trees are not the only plants in forests. Look for lichen, moss, and mushrooms. Touch some moss. Does it feel more like sandpaper or velvet? Taste some fresh, store-bought mushrooms. **Caution:** Do not eat wild mushrooms because they may be poisonous.

Thinking Skills

Develop thinking skills with the strategies outlined below.

Knowledge

Assess children's knowledge of story events with the following questions. Circle time may be used to review the story events, the seasons, and other concepts of the story. Sample questions are supplied along with answers for easy reference. Choose those that are most appropriate for your class.

1. Who plants a rainbow every year? *(Mom and I)*

2. What do they buy in fall? *(bulbs)*

3. Name some of the bulbs. *(orange tiger lily, red and orange tulips, yellow daffodil, blue hyacinth, purple crocus, purple bearded iris)*

4. What do they order from catalogs? *(seeds)*

5. What are some of the seed names? *(phlox, morning glory, zinnia, aster, cornflower, marigold, daisy)*

6. Why do they wait for spring to plant? *(so the soil will be warm enough to sprout the bulbs)*

7. What do they get at the garden center? *(seedlings)*

8. Name some of the seedlings. *(rose, poppy, delphinium, violet, pansy, fern, carnation)*

9. What colors are in the flower garden? *(red, orange, yellow, green, blue, violet)*

10. What do they do with the plants all summer? *(pick them and bring them home)*

11. What are the four seasons? *(fall, winter, spring, summer)*

12. What will happen when summer is over? *(They know they can plant another rainbow.)*

What Happens Next?

Develop comprehension skills with this lesson.

* Ask the children to tell what happens in the story after the bulbs, seeds, and seedlings are planted. (Response: *They grow.*) Ask what happens next. *(Response: We pick them.)*

* Extend the lesson. Have on hand a number of interesting pictures that you have cut out from magazines. Show one to the class and ask the children to describe what is happening in the picture. Have them tell you what will happen next.

* Try this activity when you are sure the children understand the concept before and after. Direct them to cut out a picture from a magazine. Fold a sheet of paper in half and glue the picture to the left-hand side. Tell them to draw a picture (on the right side) of what will happen next. Have them share the before-and-after pictures with a partner, a small group, or the entire class.

Circle Time

Gather the children in a circle on the floor. Choose from the following games and techniques.

Name a Flower

Materials: Bean bag or soft sponge ball

Directions:

* Ask the children to think of the name of a flower.
* Tell them that when the bean bag is tossed to them, they must name a flower.
* Toss the bean bag to a child. After a flower is named, the child tosses the bean bag back to you.
* Play continues in the same manner until all the children have had a turn naming a flower.

A Flower Is...

Directions:

* Show the class some pictures of flowers or have some live flowers on display. Discuss the characteristics of the flowers (color, size, shape, smell, etc.).
* In turn have the children complete the following sentence: A flower is...
* Follow up. Write "A flower is _____" on the chalkboard or overhead projector. Tell the children to copy and finish the sentence on a sheet of drawing paper. Have them draw a picture or write words.

What Color Is a Flower?

Directions:

* Choose one child to stand in the center of the circle.
* This child motions for another child in the circle to come into the center with him.
* The first child asks, "What color is a flower?" After the chosen child has supplied an answer, the first child goes back into the circle. The new child in the center chooses a new partner and asks the same question.
* Play continues until all the children have had a turn being in the center.
* Other questions may be substituted for "What color is a flower?" For example, "Where can you find a flower?" or "What kinds of fruits have flowers?"

Other Circle Time Activities

* Review the story events of a literature selection.
* Brainstorm lists of words such as descriptive words, flower names, color names, or places where plants grow.
* Use circle time for rhymes and rhythms.

Name _____

Bulb Matching

Directions: Cut out the bulbs at the bottom of the page. Match them to the correct shape.

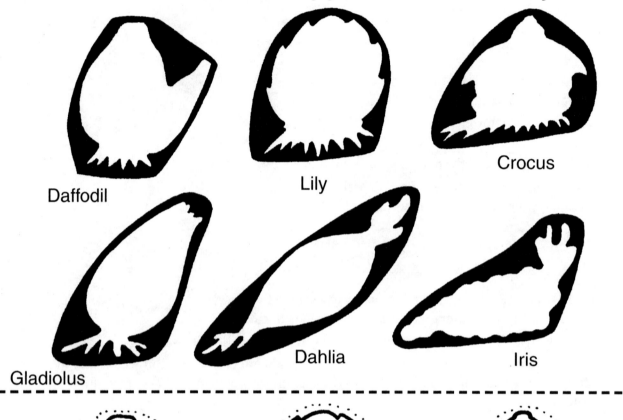

Daffodil

Lily

Crocus

Gladiolus

Dahlia

Iris

* These bulb patterns can also be used with the second activity on page 46.

Writing and Poetry

Here are four writing activities that the children will be sure to enjoy. They can share their work in small groups before taking their projects home.

Seed Packets

Materials: Seed packets, small envelopes, seeds, crayons

Directions:

* Show the class some actual seed packets. Pass them around.
* Give each child some crayons and an envelope which to draw.
* Tell children to draw seed packets for their favorite flowers.
* After the drawings are completed, put some seeds in the packets and seal the envelopes.

Original Poetry

Compose some original poetry using flower names from the story. Have the children illustrate the poems.

> **Sample:** Roses are red.
> Cornflowers are blue.
> Daffodils are yellow,
> And marigolds are too.

Couplets

With the class, brainstorm a list of flower words. Write them in a column. Next to each word write some rhyming words.

Use the words and their rhymes to write two-lined rhyming poems.

> A daffodil is a pretty yellow,
> A very happy smiling fellow.

Flower Alphabet

Read aloud the book *Alison's Zinnia* by Anita Lobel (Greenwillow Books, 1990). Children will enjoy the exquisite flowers and silly sentences contained in the book. It begins:

> "Alison acquired an Amaryllis for Beryl."
> "Beryl bought a Begonia for Crystal."

Write a class alphabet book of flower names using this same language pattern. Draw or cut out pictures from catalogs and magazines to illustrate the pages. When all the pages are complete, punch holes along one side of the pages and thread yarn through the holes. If preferred, the pages can be stapled together or assembled in a loose-leaf binder.

Extension: Lois Ehlert's *Eating the Alphabet* (Harcourt Brace Jovanovich, 1989) is a visual feast of fruits and vegetables from A to Z. Draw a class mural of fruits and vegetables.

Math Connections

All of the activities on this page are based on the text of *Planting a Rainbow.*

Counting

With the children count the number of bulbs, the number of seed packets, and the number of seedlings on the various pages of *Planting a Rainbow.*

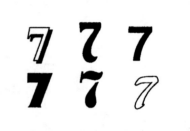

* Practice writing those numbers. For example, there are seven bulbs in the fall. Have the children write the numeral seven a number of times.

* Look for examples of that numeral in the classroom—on the clock, on a book page, or on a game piece.

Number Names

Count the number of seedlings. Establish that there are seven. Tell the children that six plus one equals seven. Can they think of any other number names for seven? (5+2, 3+4, etc.)

* Group the children and supply them with strips of paper to represent the seedlings. Have them record their answers on a sheet of paper folded into fourths. Write one addition fact in each segment.

* If appropriate, discuss the commutative property, i.e., 6 + 1 = 1 + 6; 5 + 2 = 2 + 5. Give each pair of children seven beans. Direct them to make a set of 6 and add it to a set of 1. Have them make a set of 1 and add it to a set of 6.

  =

Word Problems

Give the children props to use as you tell them a story problem. With the seed packet page, for example, you may want to supply each pair of children with a number of envelopes, library pocket cards, or actual seed packets. A sample word problem:

> "You have six seed packets." (The children make a set of six packets.) "One of you takes away two packets." (One partner physically removes two packets from the set.)

> "How many packets are left?" (They count the remaining packets.)

Continue giving the pairs word problems. Observe their actions as you walk around the classroom. Call on some children to explain the process they used.

* **Extension:** Let the children compose story problems. Pair the children and have one partner dictate a problem to the other partner. Have the children change roles. Walk around and observe the process. Ask the children to explain what they are doing and why.

A Rainbow Big Book

Culminate the topic of planting flowers with a rainbow Big Book. Two unique ideas are presented on this page. A number of flower art ideas can be found on the next page (page 56).

Overlapping Big Book

Materials: Three 9" x 12" (22 cm x 30 cm) sheets of white construction paper, a long-arm stapler, crayons

Directions:

* Place the three sheets of paper on top of one another, overlapping the ends.
* Hold the pages together about two-thirds of the way up and fold down until three overlapping pages appear above the first three pages.
* Staple on the inside fold. Fold back down and crease.
* Write red on the top section; label the others the five colors of the rainbow.
* Direct the children to draw pictures of red flowers on the red page, orange flowers on the orange page, etc.

Rainbow Pages

Materials: Six 12" x 18" (30 cm x 45 cm) sheets of white construction paper, one 8" x 12" (20 cm x 30 cm) sheet each of red, orange, yellow, green, blue, and violet construction paper, glue, stapler, scissors, tempera paints, paint brushes

Directions:

* Cut the white sheets of construction paper to the following lengths: (one each) 12" x 3" (30 x 8 cm); 12" x 6" (30 cm x 15 cm); 12" x 9" (30 cm x 23 cm); 12" x 12" (30 cm x 30 cm); 12" x 15" (30 cm x 38 cm). Do not cut the last sheet.
* Cut one 3" x 12" (8 cm x 30 cm) strip from each of the colored sheets of construction paper.
* With glue attach the red strip to the top page, the orange strip to the next page, etc.

* Label each strip with its color name.
* Assign a different page to each group of students. Tell them to paint a rainbow of flowers in the color of that page.
* When all the groups have finished their pictures, align the pages on the left side and staple together.

Innovation

Write an innovation of *Planting a Rainbow*. As a class, write about planting a desert, forest, or ocean. Make book pages as shown in either of the two methods above. Draw a different desert, forest, or ocean plant on each page.

Flowers for the Big Book

Crayons and paints work perfectly fine for illustrating Big Book pages, but if you want to try something different read through the ideas below. Look on page 57 for some flower patterns.

Layered Flowers

Materials: Colored construction paper, scissors, glue, crayons

Directions:

* Cut out a construction paper circle.

* Use another color of construction paper for the next circle which is cut smaller than the first one.

* Use a third color paper for the last circle; cut it smaller than the previous one.

* Glue the circles together, smallest on top and largest on the bottom (see diagram at right).

* Draw stem and leaf parts.

Geometric Blooms

Materials: Colored construction paper, scissors, ribbon, glue

Directions:

* Precut circles, squares, triangles, and rectangles of each color.

* Direct the children to glue geometric shapes together to construct flowers.

* Use ribbon for the stems and construction paper for the leaves.

Pipe Cleaner Creations

Materials: Colored pipe cleaners (also called chenille sticks; they are available in art supply stores), colored art chalk, glue

Directions:

* Twist the colored pipe cleaners into the desired shape.

* Attach more pipe cleaners and shape them into leaves, stems, and other flower parts.

* Glue to the page. Fill in the spaces with colored chalks.

Fabric Flowers

Materials: Fabric scraps and/or wallpaper samples, ribbon and lace trim, scissors, glue

Directions:

* Cut fabric scraps or wallpaper samples into flower and leaf shapes.

* Arrange on the page and glue the pieces down.

* Add ribbon and lace trim for the stems.

Flower Patterns

Here are some patterns for you to use when making the layered and fabric flowers on the previous page, Flowers for the Big Book. Make copies of this page onto card stock (available at photocopying facilities). Cut out around the shapes, leaving the dark outline intact. Let the children trace around the shapes onto construction paper or fabric.

Literature Connections

Use either of the two outstanding literature selections outlined below to introduce, extend, or culminate your studies about plants.

Growing Vegetable Soup by Lois Ehlert (Harcourt Brace Jovanovich, 1987)
A father and child plant seeds and sprouts, give them water, weed them, and watch them grow into vegetables. Then they dig them up, carry them home, wash them, and cook them to make vegetable soup.

Brightly colored illustrations make this book especially fun to read.

* **Step by Step.** As a class, review the steps the father and child followed to grow and cook the vegetables. Write each step on a separate strip of paper to be used on a pocket chart. Have pairs of children work together to arrange the strips in correct chronological order.

* **Make Vegetable Soup.** Enlist parent help to supply the vegetables and supervision in preparing and cooking the vegetables. While the soup is cooking, read aloud Marcia Brown's *Stone Soup* (Scribner, 1947).

* **Vegetable Sculptures.** You will need raw carrots, radishes, jicama, celery, zucchini, and other vegetables, toothpicks and tiny marshmallows, raisins, pickles, olives, or other garnishes. With pieces of toothpick attach garnishes to the vegetables to make sculptures or funny faces.

Miss Rumphius by Barbara Cooney (Viking Press, 1982)
Miss Rumphius is a librarian who decides to travel the world. She has a number of wonderful adventures from the jungles to the pyramids. When she settles into her New England home she wants to make the world more beautiful. Her plan is to plant a garden of lupines. Every year they continue to grow.

* **Pressed Flowers.** Let each child place a flower between two sheets of newspaper. Pile some heavy books on top. Wait at least two weeks before removing the books and newspaper.

* **Scenes.** Divide the class into four groups. Assign each group a different setting—jungle, tropical island, desert, snow-covered mountain. Have each group create a mural showing something Miss Rumphius might have done in that locale. Display the four completed murals side by side.

* **Circle Time.** Discuss ways that they could make the school more beautiful. As a class choose one project on which to work on.

* **Reading.** The state flower of Texas is the bluebonnet, which is from the same family as the lupine. Read aloud *Legend of the Bluebonnet* by Tomie dePaola (Putnam Publishing Group, 1983). If possible, display a bouquet of bluebonnets.

A Tree Is Nice
by Janice May Udry

Summary

There are any number of reasons why trees are nice and author Janice May Udry has explored them in a most effective fashion. In words and pictures she takes the reader through a seasonal journey in the life of a tree. Each page treats its readers to different reasons why trees are nice. As you read this book you can almost hear a child's voice saying, "Trees are very nice. They fill up the sky."

First published in 1956 this Caldecott Medal winner is timeless in its subject matter. All children will be able to relate to this pleasant story because trees affect us all. They provide us with oxygen, food, and materials for clothing and shelter. They can give us hours of enjoyment, and they are beautiful to see. This book is a good introduction to a unit on trees through the seasons.

Overview of Activities

Setting the Stage

Walking Tour. Go outside for a walking tour and really take a look at the trees in the neighborhood. Ask the children to describe them. Talk about things they can do with trees. Back in the classroom the children can draw pictures of trees.

The Four Seasons. Briefly discuss the changes that occur during each season. Talk about the different clothes they wear as the temperatures change (jackets and mittens in winter, bathing suits in summer, etc). Make some season people (on page 61).

Trees. Establish that plants change throughout the seasons, too. Use a tree as an example. How does it look in the spring, summer, etc.? Discuss the changes that take place. Show the children pictures of a tree during each of the seasons. *The Tree* by Gallimard Jeunesse (Scholastic, 1989) is an excellent resource for this activity. (See the Bibliography on page 80 for more suggested titles.)

A Hand-Y Tree. Make trees to reflect the current season and each subsequent one. Children trace around their hands or make hand prints to create the trees. Complete directions are on page 62.

Poems. Read aloud the poem "Our Tree" by Marchette Chute. (It can be found in *Sing a Song of Popcorn,* selected by Beatrice Schenck de Regniers, Scholastic, Inc., 1988.) This beautiful verse describes the changes in an apple tree through the seasons. Another good read-aloud is Karla Kuskin's "The Tree and Me" from her book *Dogs & Dragons Trees & Dreams* (Harper Trophy, 1980).

Overview of Activities *(cont.)*

Enjoying the Story

Seasonal Tree. Create a seasonal tree (directions are on page 61) and add the suggested decorations according to the season. Display it all year long and change its decor as necessary.

Story Activities. From circle time to role-playing, the activities on page 64 will develop vocabulary and reinforce concepts from the story. Children can make a leaf crown (see page 65) to wear during some of these projects.

Language Experiences. Five different methods for expanding language skills are outlined on page 66. Patterns for making *A Tree Is Nice* book can be found on pages 67 and 68.

Movement and Songs. In the first activity on page 69 the children become trees through the seasons. The second activity is an old song with new words. You may want to make up your own verses.

Art Projects. Explore the seasons with art projects especially designed for each one. Page 70 has directions for four easy-to-do crafts.

Science. Find out more about trees growing in different habitats. Collect leaves and compare them. Learn how roots carry water up through their stems to their leaves and/or examine the veins on a leaf. Directions for these can be found on page 71, Tree Science.

Math. Ideas for leaf matching, making games for the children, and how to use leaves as props can all be found on page 72, Tree Math. Use those ideas which best suit your classroom needs.

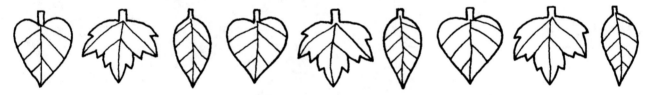

Extending the Story

Food Fun. What better way to learn about trees than with some cooking projects! At least one of the five easy-to-make treats on page 73 is sure to please even the most finicky eater.

Literature Connections. Read some other books about trees. Two wonderful picture books are named on page 74, along with some suggested related activities. Other titles to explore include the following:

* *The Giving Tree* by Shel Silverstein (Harper & Row, 1964)
  A small boy loves a tree, and as a child he visits it daily. As he grows up their relationship changes.

* *Ten Tall Oaktrees* by Richard Edwards (Tambourine Books, 1988)
  This is the tale of what happens to a grove of trees as the world around them develops housing and industry.

Other Trees. Learn about trees that do not lose their leaves. Compare a palm tree with a maple tree. How are the leaves different? Write an innovation of *A Tree Is Nice* substituting a palm tree or Joshua tree for the one in the story. Read *Cactus in the Desert* by Phyllis A. Busch (Thomas Y. Crowell, 1979) for background information.

Through the Seasons

Seasonal Tree

Materials: Bare tree branch (small), old paint bucket or other container, plaster of paris

Directions:

* Mix the plaster of paris according to directions.
* Pour into the container. Stand the branch up in the center and hold it upright until the plaster sets.
* Add decorations according to the seasons. Make paper cutouts, dough ornaments, or use real artifacts. Some suggestions:

FALL: leaves, Halloween pumpkins, Thanksgiving turkeys

WINTER: snow, Valentines, shamrocks, Presidents' Day flags

SPRING: eggs, rabbits, flowers, birds' nests, umbrellas, buds

SUMMER: fruit, kites, boats, suns

Season People

Materials: Butcher paper, dark marking pen, scissors, crayons or paints

Directions:

* Spread the butcher paper flat on the floor. Have the child lie down on top of the paper.
* With the marking pen trace the child's outline.
* Cut out. Make four of these people patterns.
* Divide the class into four groups. Direct the groups to "dress" their persons for different seasons; i.e., suggest the fall group draw a sweater and long pants on their person; the winter group design snow boots, jacket, and mittens; the spring group create a raincoat and rain boots; the summer group draw a bathing suit or shorts outfit on their person.
* Attach the seasonal people on the wall next to one another.
* One group at a time can tell why they dressed their person in those kinds of clothes. You may also want them to explain what changes are occurring in trees and plants during that season.

Season Watch

Materials: Chart paper, marking pen

Directions:

* At the beginning of each season go for a nature walk.
* Tell the children to be aware of signs of that particular season.
* On chart paper, write the children's responses to the question "What signs of _____(season) did you see or hear?" (A spring response might be, "I saw a robin making a nest." A fall response could be, "The leaves on the trees are changing colors."
* Refer to the list of responses made on the chart paper activity. Have the children copy one word, sentence, or phrase of their choice from that list and draw a picture or write a seasonal story.

A Tree Through the Seasons

Read aloud *The Gift of the Tree* by Alvin Tresselt (Lothrop, Lee & Shepard, 1992). Follow up with a class flow chart of story events or a life cycle chart, using paper plates. Write one event on each plate. Attach the plates to a wall in correct chronological order. Connect them with craft yarn.

A Hand-y Tree

Introduce your studies of plants through the seasons with this hand-y art project. Each one begins with a hand outline, but a different art activity is suggested to represent each season.

The Basic Tree

Materials: Brown tempera paint, white drawing paper, paintbrushes, shallow pan

Directions:

* Pour the brown tempera paint into a shallow pan.

* Have the child place one hand over the surface of the paint.

* Direct the child to spread his/her fingers as they press onto the white construction paper to make a basic print.

* After cleaning the paint off their hands, the children can use brushes to paint tree trunks.

* Allow plenty of time for the pictures to dry. Use any of the seasonal ideas which follow.

Variations:

1. Tell the child to place one hand on a sheet of white drawing paper with fingers spread out a little. With a brown marking pen, trace around the hand (including the individual fingers). Have the child color the branches brown and draw a tree trunk.

2. Use the tree pattern on page 63. Color, cut out, and glue to a white background.

SUMMER TREES

* Cut out green squares of construction paper. Glue to the branches to make leafy summer trees.

* Cut sponges into leaf shapes. Dip the leaf into green tempera paint and stamp a number of leaves on each branch.

FALL TREES

* Dip cotton puffs or cotton swabs into red, orange, and yellow tempera paint. Make dabs of paint on the tree branches for fall leaves.

* Color your own cotton puffs. Make red, orange, and yellow in separate bags. Place a bunch of puffs in a plastic bag along with one-fourth cup of dry tempera powder. Shake well. Then glue the colored puffs to the paper.

WINTER TREES

* Glue foam packing pieces or dried eggshell pieces to the branches.

* With white chalk, trace a tree and trunk shape onto black construction paper. Draw snow on the branches.

SPRING TREES

* Cut out squares of pink, red, and yellow art tissue. Direct the children to roll up each square into a ball. Glue a number of these tissue balls to the ends of the branches.

* With a hole punch make pink, red, and yellow circles. Have the children glue these to the ends of the tree branches to make buds.

Tree Pattern

* For suggested uses see pages 62 and 66.

Story Activities

These activities will help encourage vocabulary development and reinforce concepts from *A Tree Is Nice*. Choose those which are most appropriate for your group of children.

Review

* During circle time review all the things the characters said about trees—children played in the leaves, children sat on a limb and thought, birds built nests in them, they made shade, they helped keep people cool, etc. After your discussion, direct the children to draw pictures of one of those events.

* One at a time have them share their pictures with the others in the class.

Pictures

* Closely observe the tree during different seasons. How do the leaves look in fall? How are they different from summer leaves? Look through some nature magazines and find pictures of leaves during the different seasons.

Role Playing

* Explore some of the things that the characters did with the trees in fall. For example, they played in the piles of leaves and built playhouses out of them. If possible, go outside and enact these scenes. If no leaves are available, make some (see patterns on page 65) out of construction paper. Let pairs or small groups act out these and other scenes from the story.

* In the summer the characters in the story find sticks from trees and use them to draw in the sand. The children can draw pictures with sticks in the sand box. For individual boxes fill a shoe box lid or other shallow container with cornmeal. The children can draw pictures in the cornmeal "sand" with small twigs.

* People have picnics in the shade of a tree. Take the children outdoors and sit in the shade of a tree while enjoying a snack.

Planting a Tree

* Plant an outdoor class tree. Visit a local nursery to learn about trees and how to plant them. Enlist outside help to plant larger trees. (Children may be able to plant seedlings with only your help.) Label the tree with a flag or some kind of sign containing the date, type of tree, and names of all the students who participated in the project.

* Review the steps necessary to plant a tree. Write each step on a different strip of paper. Use with a pocket chart and have the children arrange the steps in correct chronological order.

* An excellent picture book about how to plant a tree is Lois Ehlert's *Red Leaf, Yellow Leaf* (Harcourt Brace Jovanovich, 1991). Share the pictures and story with the children. Read the text in the last pages to help you with your tree planting lessons.

* Keep some potted trees in the classroom. Assign different children to take care of watering every day or week. Observe each tree's growth over a period of time. (See page 11, Plant Reports, for some ideas about observation charts.)

Leaf Crown

Materials: Copies of the leaf patterns below, crayons, scissors, glue, construction paper strips, stapler

Directions:

* Have the children color and cut out a number of leaves.
* Staple two strips of construction paper together to make a circle to fit the child's head.
* Glue or staple the leaves to the crown.
* Wear while doing any of the movements described on page 69. The leaf patterns can also be used with the role-playing activity on page 64.
* **Note:** Real leaves can be used in place of these paper patterns.

Language Experiences

Build and expand language skills and vocabulary with any of these lessons.

Discussion. Talk about trees and why they are nice. Write a language pattern on the board for the children to copy and fill in. They may use vocabulary from the story or words of their own.

> Sample: Trees are nice. They _____.
> They go beside _____ and down _____.
> They live up on the _____.

A Tree Is Nice Book. Expand on the discussion above with a book. (Two different sample pages can be found on pages 67 and 68.) Review the four seasons briefly. Talk about how trees change through the seasons.

* Make enough photocopies of either page (or design your own) for each child.
* The children can dictate or write endings to each sentence.
* Direct the children to illustrate each sentence.
* Cut out the pages on the solid lines.
* Make a construction paper cover and staple all the pages together.
* Pair the children and let them practice reading their books to each other.

The Four Seasons. Gather the children around you. Draw a circle on chart paper and divide it into fourths. Write the name of a season in each segment. Read the poem "Four Seasons" aloud to the children. Ask them for words to describe each season and write them in the proper segments on the circle.

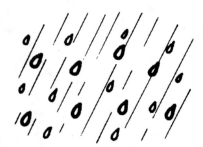

Four Seasons

Spring is showery, flowery, bowery.
Summer: hoppy, croppy, poppy.
Autumn: wheezy, sneezy, freezy.
Winter: slippy, drippy, nippy.
– Author unknown

Tree Products. Use circle time to talk about the different things we get from trees—fruits, nuts, wood for building, etc. Give each child a copy of the tree pattern (see page 63). Direct the class to look through old magazines for pictures of things we get from trees. Have them cut out the pictures and glue one to each branch. If you prefer, the children may draw pictures or write words on the branches.

It Could Still Be a Tree. Allan Fowler's photo essay—*It Could Still Be a Tree* (Children's Press, 1990)—explains how to tell whether a plant is a tree. Even though a palm has broad leaves, it is still a tree, for example. Have the children write their own beginnings to fit this language pattern:

_____ it could still be a tree.

A Tree Is Nice Book

* See page 66 for directions.

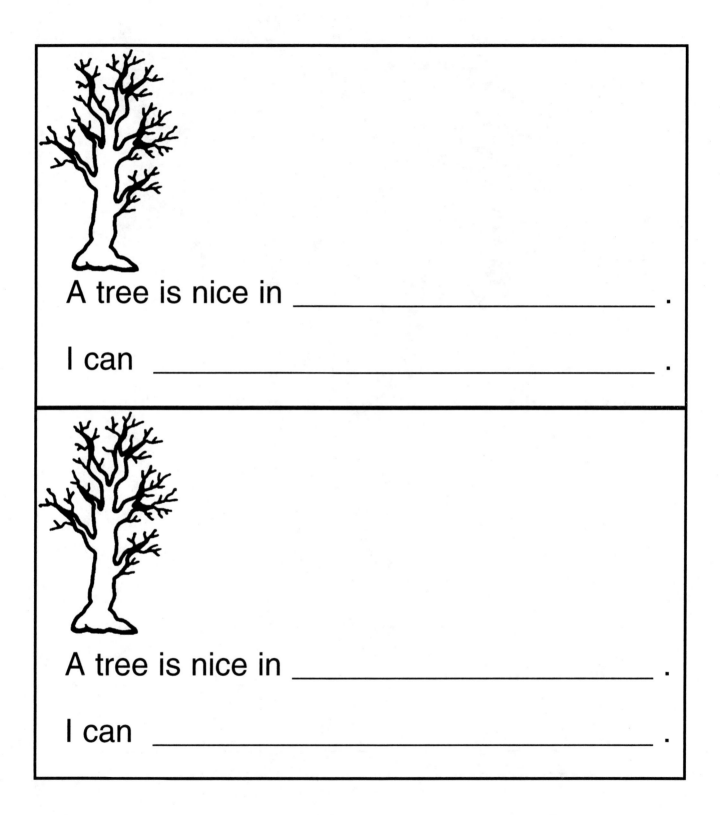

A tree is nice in _____ .

I can _____ .

A tree is nice in _____ .

I can _____ .

A Tree Is Nice Book *(cont.)*

A tree is nice in _____ .

I can _____

_____ .

Movement and Songs

A Tree Through the Seasons

* Set the mood with appropriate background music.

* Describe a scene so that the children can see a picture in their minds.

* Encourage the use of props.

* Suggested movements for each season:

Summer

* A bird is building a nest in your uppermost branches. (Pair the children. One partner is the tree swaying slowly, happily. The other partner is the bird building a nest in the other's hair. Use cotton, small twigs, and fabric scraps. Trade roles.)

Fall

* The wind is beginning to sway your branches. Your leaves are falling off. (Give each child a number of paper leaves or let them make their own. Have them sway and drop their leaves.)

Winter

* It is very cold outside now. Snow is falling on your branches. (Pair the children. One partner is the tree; arms are extended and the body is shivering. The other partner drapes snow, use white yarn or fabric on the outstretched arms. Have the children exchange roles.).

Spring

* Days are getting warmer now. Buds are beginning to open on your branches. (Children keep their arms at their sides as they dance joyfully. Slowly they open their hands to show the buds opening.)

A Palm Tree During a Tropical Rain Storm

* The rain is coming down slowly and splashing on all your branches. Now the rain is hitting you harder and harder. (Give each child a section of newspaper. Tell them to hold the paper with both hands as they wave it through the air faster and faster to make rain sounds.)

Here We Go Round the Mulberry Bush

* Sing and play a game of "Here We Go Round the Mulberry Bush." Music for this song can be found in *Tom Glazer's Treasury of Songs for Children* (compiled by Tom Glazer, Doubleday, 1964).

* Substitute other tree names for mulberry bush—Joshua tree, cypress tree, cottonwood tree, etc.

* Make up your own verses or use some of the following ideas.

> This is how the leaves fall off, the leaves fall off, the leaves fall off.
> This is how the leaves fall off, all autumn long.
> (One child is the tree. The others can hold handfuls of real or paper leaves and drop them as they sing and dance around the tree.)
> This is how the branches sway, branches sway, branches sway.
> This is how the branches sway, all during spring.
> (The children can move their arms gracefully as they sing this verse.)

Art Projects Through the Seasons

On this page you will find four art projects to accompany each seasonal change. Modify as needed.

WINTER: Brown Branches

Materials: Liquid brown tempera paint, brushes, drawing paper, white art chalk

Directions:

* Place a blob of liquid brown tempera paint onto the middle of the drawing paper.
* Each child brushes the paint from the center to form branches.
* After the paint has dried, draw a layer of snow onto the branches with white chalk.

SPRING: *Thumbprint Blossoms*

Materials: Sponges, liquid pink tempera paint (mix white with red), white drawing paper, green crayons

Directions:

* Pour some tempera paint over the surface of the sponge.
* Direct the child to place one thumb in the pink paint on the sponge.
* Make a cluster of thumbprints onto the drawing paper.
* With green crayon draw leaves.

Variation: Use popped popcorn for the blossoms. Draw leaves.

SUMMER: Framed Fruit

Materials: Wallpaper samples, plaid or other colorful fabric scraps, glue, white construction paper, shoebox lid, scissors, craft yarn, one hole punch

Directions:

* Cut a piece of construction paper to fit inside the lid and glue it on.
* Cut fruit shapes out of wallpaper and fabric.
* Arrange onto the lid background. Glue down.
* Punch one hole on each side of the lid near the top (see diagram).
* Tie a knot in one end of a length of yarn and thread it through one hole.
* Thread the other end through the second hole, tie a knot.
* Hang up the fruit designs.

FALL: Stenciled Leaves

Materials: Real leaves (or use the leaf patterns on page 65), paintbrush, liquid tempera paints in orange, yellow, red, and brown, white drawing paper

Directions:

* Place a leaf anywhere on the paper. Hold it in place with one hand.
* With the other hand paint short strokes away from the edge of the leaf all around its shape.
* Move the leaf to another area of the paper. Repeat the painting process. Make as many shapes as desired on a page.

Tree Science

The ideas on this page can be used to introduce, reinforce, or extend concepts about trees.

Tree Types

Learn about other kinds of trees that grow in different habitats, e.g., Joshua and palm trees of the desert, spruce and fir of the forests, etc. Look at pictures of different trees in their habitats. Stunningly beautiful photos can be found in *It Could Still Be a Tree* by Allan Fowler (Children's Press, 1990). Another fine resource is *Seasons* by Illa Podendorf (Children's Press, 1981). This picture book shows what happens to tropical, desert, and other trees through the seasons.

Leaf Collection

Ask the children to bring in some fallen leaves from trees. Collect and compare all the leaves.

* Count them. Use the leaves to make sets.
* Classify them. Group the children. Have them divide the leaves into groups according to color, size, and shape.
* Learn about three different kinds of leaf edges-smooth, toothed, and lobed. Have the children identify these leaf types. Encourage them to use the words "smooth," "toothed," and "lobed."

Veins

Talk about the function of leaves (they make food for the tree) and their veins (they carry water into the leaf). Examine leaves closely with a magnifying glass. Make leaf rubbings.

Materials: Variety of leaves, crayons or soft lead pencils, thin white tracing paper or typing paper
Directions:
* Distribute the leaves to the children.
* Tell them to place a sheet of paper over the leaf. Check to make sure that the vein side is up.
* With a crayon or pencil lightly rub over the whole surface of the leaf. Observe the patterns.

Variation: Using the same procedure, make bark rubbings.

Roots

Establish that the purpose of the roots is to draw water up from the ground. In turn, the trunk carries the water up through the roots to the leaves. To demonstrate that a root carries water through its entire stem, do the following experiment.

Materials: Food coloring, two clear vases filled with water, white Queen Anne's lace, carnations, or other type of flowers (White carnations will produce the most dramatic results.)
Directions:
* Add a few drops of food coloring to the water in one vase, stir to mix.
* Leave the water in the other vase clear.
* Place some flowers in each vase.
* Observe the flowers over the next few days. The ones in the colored water will absorb the coloring, while the other flowers will remain the same color.

Tree Math

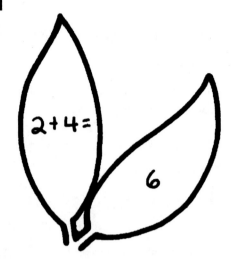

Leaf Matching

Make six copies of the patterns on page 65. Glue the patterns to colored tagboard, laminate, and cut out. Write a different equation on each of nine leaves. Label the remaining leaves with the corresponding answers. Have pairs of children work together to match the equations with the answers. These leaf cards may also be used to match like sets, like numbers, or number names with numerals (see examples).

Props

Collect a number of leaves from outdoors or make your own out of construction paper (see the patterns on page 65). Give each child a dozen leaves. Have them manipulate the leaves as you relay story problems. For example, "Four leaves fall off of a tree." Child makes a set of four leaves. "Three more leaves fall from the tree. How many leaves are there altogether?" Child makes a set of three leaves and adds it to the set of four leaves. Continue in the same manner with other problems.

Weighing

You will need a balance scale for this activity. Place an apple on one side of the scale. Ask the children how many marbles (blocks, washers, or any other unit of measurement you want to use) it will take to balance the scale. Record the estimates. Count as you add weights to balance the scale. Repeat the process with different sizes of apples and different units of measurement.

Tree Sets

For this project you will need 20 small, unlined index cards (or cut your own rectangles from construction paper or colored tagboard), a stamp pad, a tree stamp, and a green marking pen. Divide the cards into two groups. On the first group of cards write a numeral from one to ten. On the second group of cards stamp a set of one to ten trees on each card. Individuals or pairs of students can practice matching the sets to the numerals. Store the cards in a labeled manila envelope.

Story Board

Make a copy of page 68 (cover up the text before copying) and glue to heavy paper. Color, laminate, and cut out. Cut out a number of brown construction paper circles for coconuts. Tell a story and have the child manipulate the pieces. For example, "There were seven coconuts in the tree." The child makes a set of seven coconuts in the tree. "Four coconuts fell to the ground. How many were left in the tree?" Child moves four coconuts to the ground and counts three in the tree.

Food Fun

Learn more about trees with these unique treats, some of them homemade!

Food from Trees

Most children will know that some fruit comes from trees. What other edible products come from trees? Have a tasting party. Bring in maple syrup, walnuts, pecans, coconuts, cashews, and other nuts for the children to sample. If possible, have shelled and unshelled nuts of each variety for the children to compare. **Note:** If children in your class are very young, you may prefer to omit the nut tasting. Check for any food allergies.

A Broccoli Tree

Some adult help may be required for this project, so invite family members to participate in this cooking lesson.

Ingredients: Broccoli florets, carrots, parsley

Utensils: Knives, paper plates

Directions:

*   * Wash the broccoli florets and the parsley; set aside.
*   * Peel the carrots. Cut them into thin strips; cut in half.
*   * Arrange two or three carrot strips side by side on the paper plate.
*   * At the top of the carrot strips, arrange a cluster of broccoli florets.
*   * Along the bottom of the carrot strips, make a layer of parsley grass. (See diagram.)
*   * Eat the broccoli trees plain or dip the vegetables into ranch dressing (or unflavored yogurt).

Gelatin Trees

Prepare lime gelatin according to the package directions for recipe for reduced liquid. Pour into a large pan so that a thin layer is formed. After it has set, cut out trees with a tree-shaped cookie cutter. Eat the lime trees.

Tree Sandwiches

Make peanut butter and jelly sandwiches. Cut out tree shapes with a cookie cutter.

Tree Cookies

Buy prepared cookie dough at the grocery store. Give each child a small handful of dough. Add extra flour as this dough will get very sticky as children work with it.

*   * Make a thumb print in the center of the dough.
*   * Add two or three drops of food coloring.
*   * Show the children how to knead the coloring into the dough.
*   * They can roll the dough and cut out tree shapes with cookie cutters. Add cookie decorations (optional).

Variation: Pair the children. Give one partner in each pair brown food coloring to make a tree trunk. Provide the other partner with green food coloring to make leaves, fronds, etc. Bake as directed.

Literature Connections

Use either of the two outstanding literature selections outlined below to introduce, extend, or culminate your studies about trees.

"Trees" a poem by Harry Behn (Henry Holt and Company, 1949)

> "Trees are the kindest things I know,
> They do no harm, they simply grow."

So begins a most eloquent poem about why trees are important. It was first copyrighted many years ago (1949,) but the words are just as meaningful today as then. Thought-provoking pictures give added definition to the text. Overall, it is an enticing picture book for young and old alike.

* **Language Pattern.** Write the first sentence of the poem—Trees are the kindest things I know... on chart paper. Tell the children to copy it onto a sheet of paper and finish the sentence with their own words. (Some children may have to dictate their words to you.) Have them draw a picture to go along with the text.

* **Trees Give Us...** During circle time discuss what the poem says trees give us (shade for sleepy cows, birds among their boughs, fruit, wood to make houses, leaves to burn on Halloween, green buds). Write each phrase on a separate sheet of paper. Group the children and direct them to draw pictures to illustrate the words. Compile all the pages into a Trees Give Us... class book.

* **Tree Types.** Observe and identify the different kinds of trees in the pictures of the book. Do any of these kinds of trees grow in your area? Tell the children to draw a typical tree found in their neighborhoods.

The Seasons of Arnold's Apple Tree by Gail Gibbons (Harcourt Brace Jovanovich, 1984)

Arnold watches his tree change as it goes through the seasons. In the spring buds begin to grow. Arnold builds a swing and weaves an apple blossom wreath. When summer comes the apples have turned green. He builds a tree house to play in. By fall the apples have turned red, and the leaves on the tree are a bright array of colors. His family makes apple pie and apple cider. Winter brings snow to Arnold's bare tree. He builds a snow fort and a snowman. Slowly the snow melts; it is spring once again.

* Treat the children to apple pie or apple cider as they listen to you read this story.

* **Fractions.** Explore simple fractions with an apple. Cut it into halves and then fourths.

* **Easy as Applesauce.** To make four small servings of applesauce, peel and core four small, sweet apples. Cut into one inch (2.54 cm), or smaller, pieces and place into a saucepan along with $^1/_2$ cup (125 mL) of water. Cook over medium heat, stirring occasionally until apples are tender. Mash with a potato masher and mix in $^1/_2$ tsp. (2.5 mL) of cinnamon. Spoon into little paper souffle cups so each child can sample the applesauce.

Rainbow of Flowers

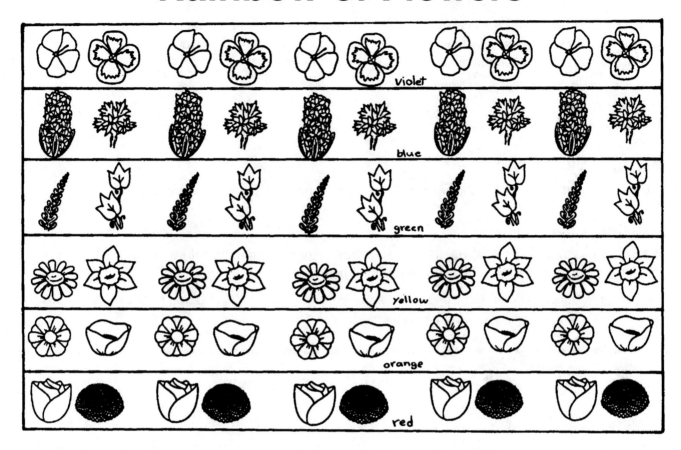

This multifunctional bulletin board is an eye-catching display as well as an interactive teaching tool. To construct the bulletin board, follow the directions below. To create learning games, make two more sets of flower patterns on white paper and another set on colored paper. Game directions follow on page 76.

Purposes:

1. To stimulate interest in flowers

2. To use as an interactive teaching tool

Materials: White butcher paper, red, orange, yellow, green, blue, and purple construction paper, scissors, flower patterns from pages 77 to 79, stapler, green craft yarn (optional)

Directions:

1. Line the bulletin board background with white butcher paper.

2. With a paper cutter or scissors, cut ¾" (2 cm) construction paper strips of each color.

3. Assemble the strips onto the bulletin board as shown in the diagram.

4. Copy the flower patterns (pages 77 to 79) onto construction paper and cut out. (Make as many copies as you will need.)

5. Arrange the flowers onto the corresponding rows.

6. Optional—If your bulletin board space is large enough, use craft yarn to create stems. Then cut out green construction paper leaves (see the leaf patterns on the bottom of page 76).

Games

To make the Rainbow of Flowers Bulletin Board an interactive one just make extra copies of the flower patterns on pages 77 to 79. For the first game, make one set of colored flowers. You will need two sets of white flowers for the remaining games.

Matching Like Colors

Have the children match the colored flowers to the correct row on the bulletin board.

Matching Like Shapes

Use a set of white flowers for this game. The child matches the shape to the correct flower.

Matching Color Names

Make a set of white flowers. Write its corresponding color name, on the colored flower. Have the child match the color names to the colors on the bulletin board.

Variation: Write each color name on a separate index card. Direct the children to match the color name with the correct section of the bulletin board.

- -

Leaf Patterns

For directions see page 75.

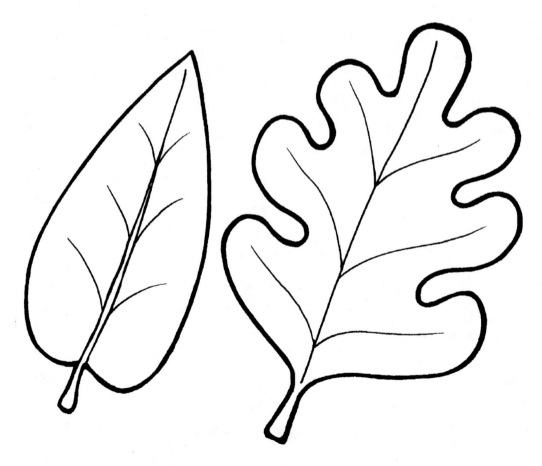

Bulletin Board Patterns

red tulip

red carnation

orange zinnia

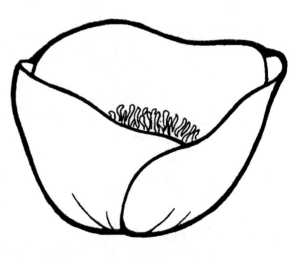

orange poppy

Bulletin Board Patterns *(cont.)*

yellow daisy

yellow daffodil

green fern

green ivy

Bulletin Board Patterns *(cont.)*

blue hyacinth

blue cornflowers

purple violet

purple pansy

Bibliography

Literature

Aliki. *Corn Is Maize.* HarperCollins, 1976.

Aliki. *Johnny Appleseed.* Prentice-Hall, 1963.

Behn, Harry. *Trees.* Henry Holt and Company, Inc., 1949.

Brown, Marc. *Your First Garden Book.* Little, Brown and Company, 1981.

Busch, Phyllis A. *Cactus in the Desert.* Thomas Y. Crowell, 1979.

Cooney, Barbara. *Miss Rumphius.* Viking Press, 1982.

dePaola, Tomie. *The Popcorn Book.* Holiday, 1978.

Edwards, Richard. *Ten Tall Oaktrees.* Tambourine Books, 1988.

Ehlert, Lois. *Eating the Alphabet.* Harcourt Brace Jovanovich, 1989.

Ehlert, Lois. *Growing Vegetable Soup.* Harcourt Brace Jovanovich, 1987.

Ehlert, Lois. *Planting a Rainbow.* Harcourt Brace Jovanovich, 1988.

Ehlert, Lois. *Red Leaf, Yellow Leaf.* Harcourt Brace Jovanovich, 1991.

Galdone, Paul. *Jack and the Beanstalk.* Clarion, 1982.

Gibbons, Gail. *The Seasons of Arnold's Apple Tree.* Harcourt Brace Jovanovich, 1984.

Guiberson, Brenda Z. *Cactus Hotel.* Henry Holt and Company, 1991.

Heller, Ruth. *Plants that Never Ever Bloom.* Grosset & Dunlap, 1984.

Heller, Ruth. *The Reason for a Flower.* Putnam & Grossett, 1983.

Horton, Barbara Savadge. *What Comes in Spring?* Alfred A. Knopf, 1992.

Jordan, Helene J. *How a Seed Grows.* Harper Trophy, 1992.

Kellogg, Steven. *Johnny Appleseed.* Morrow, 1988.

Krauss, Ruth. *The Carrot Seed.* HarperCollins Children's Books, 1945.

Lindbergh, Reeve. *Johnny Appleseed.* Little, Brown and Company, 1990.

Maestro, Betsy. *How Do Apples Grow?* Harper Trophy, 1992.

Manson, Christopher, adapted by. *The Tree in the Wood.* North/South Books, 1993.

Schotter, Roni. *Fruit & Vegetable Man.* Little, Brown and Company, 1993.

Silverstein, Shel. *The Giving Tree.* Harper & Row, 1964.

Titherington, Jeanne. *Pumpkin Pumpkin.* Mulberry Books, 1986.

Tresselt, Alvin. *The Gift of the Tree.* Lothrop, Lee & Shepard, 1992.

Udry, Janice May. *A Tree Is Nice.* Harper Trophy, 1956.

Wexler, Jerome. *Flowers Fruits Seeds.* Simon & Schuster, 1987.

Poetry

Brown, Margaret Wise. *Under the Sun and the Moon and Other Poems*

Kuskin, Karla. *Dogs & Dragons Trees & Dreams.* Harper Trophy, 198

O'Neill, Mary. *Hailstones and Halibut Bones.* Delacorte Press, 1961.

Schenck de Regniers, Beatrice, selected by. *Sing a Song of Popcorn.* S

Teacher Created Resources

#266 *Apples—A Thematic Unit*

#263 *Popcorn—A Thematic Unit*

#251 *Seasons—A Thematic Unit*

#346 *Connecting Art and Literature*

Multimedia

W. Atlee Burpee Company, famous for its seeds and garden prod
children's seed-growing campaign. For $3 you can order a
seeds. Write to Grow America, Premium Division, W. Atl
Warminster, PA 18974.

What Is a Seed ? (National Geographic Educational Services, 199
seeds travel and grow. It is for primary students and costs
information.